REASONING FROM THE SCRIPTURES

SHARING CHRIST AS YOU HELP OTHERS TO LEARN ABOUT THE MIGHTY WORKS OF GOD

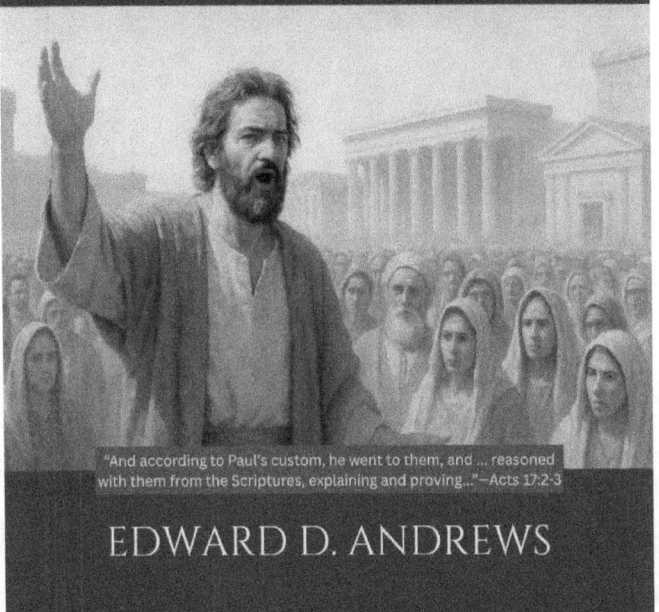

"And according to Paul's custom, he went to them, and ... reasoned with them from the Scriptures, explaining and proving..." —Acts 17:2-3

EDWARD D. ANDREWS

REASONING FROM The SCRIPTURES

Sharing CHRIST as You Help Others to Learn about the Mighty Works of God

Edward D. Andrews

Christian Publishing House

Cambridge, Ohio

Copyright © 2025 Edward D. Andrews

All rights reserved. Except for brief quotations in articles, other publications, book reviews, and blogs, no part of this book may be reproduced in any manner without prior written permission from the publishers. For information, write,

support@christianpublishers.org

REASONING FROM The SCRIPTURES: Sharing CHRIST as You Help Others to Learn about the Mighty Works of God by Edward D. Andrews

ISBN-10: 1945757825

ISBN-13: 978-1945757822

Table of Contents

Preface 7

INTRODUCTION 9

CHAPTER 1 Evangelism: The Divine Mandate to Proclaim the Good News 14

CHAPTER 2 Evangelism: Proclaiming the Kingdom of God in a World of Darkness 23

CHAPTER 3 The Art of Evangelism: Proclaiming Truth with Wisdom, Courage, and Compassion 34

CHAPTER 4 The Role of Scripture in Evangelism: The Power of God's Word to Convict, Convert, and Transform 45

CHAPTER 5 The Character of the Evangelist: Reflecting Christ in Word, Life, and Witness 56

CHAPTER 6 Understanding Your Audience: The Wisdom of Reaching Hearts Through Truth. 67

CHAPTER 7 All True Christians Are Evangelizers: The Divine Calling of Every Follower of Christ 78

CHAPTER 8 Starting Your Evangelism Journey as a Beginner: Learning to Share the Gospel with Confidence and Faithfulness 89

CHAPTER 9 Street-Level Witness: Sharing Faith in Everyday Encounters 101

CHAPTER 10 Digital Disciples: Evangelism in the Age of Social Media 114

CHAPTER 11 Overcoming Fear: Bold Steps to Proclaim the Good News 126

CHAPTER 12 Building Bridges: Connecting with Skeptics and Seekers 137

CHAPTER 13 Answering Objections: Equipping Yourself for Common Challenges 149

CHAPTER 14 Evangelizing Like Jesus Christ 163

CHAPTER 15 Evangelizing Like the Apostle Paul: Reasoning, Explaining, Proving, and Persuading with the Gospel 175

Glossary of Terms 189

Bibliography 198

Preface

The heart of Christianity beats through evangelism—the proclamation of the good news that God has acted in history through His Son, Jesus Christ, to redeem a fallen world. Yet in every generation, this sacred task faces new challenges: skepticism, apathy, false religion, and distraction. The need for believers who can *reason from the Scriptures*—clearly, courageously, and compassionately—has never been greater.

This book, *Reasoning from the Scriptures*, was written to equip every follower of Christ to proclaim the truth of the gospel with confidence and conviction. Its purpose is not merely to inform but to transform—to strengthen the believer's understanding of God's Word and to inspire obedience to the Great Commission. Evangelism is not a duty assigned to a few; it is the divine calling of all who have been redeemed by grace.

Each chapter draws upon the timeless principles of Scripture and the examples of the Master Evangelist, Jesus Christ, and His faithful servant, the Apostle Paul. Readers will find guidance on proclaiming the gospel in a world of confusion, engaging skeptics with truth, overcoming fear, and building bridges of compassion toward those who do not yet know the Savior. The goal is to blend sound doctrine with practical wisdom so that every believer may speak truth with both clarity and love.

The phrase "reasoning from the Scriptures" captures the essence of biblical evangelism. The apostles did not depend on emotional persuasion or clever rhetoric; they opened the Word of God and demonstrated that Jesus is the promised Christ. In our own time, the same method remains our sure foundation. The Bible is not only the message of salvation—it is the means by which the Spirit convicts, converts, and transforms hearts.

This work continues a lifelong pursuit of helping Christians know, defend, and declare the truth. It is offered with the prayer that Jehovah will use it to stir renewed passion for evangelism, strengthen confidence in His Word, and call many to faith in His Son. May it encourage you to see every conversation, every question, and every encounter as an opportunity to point someone to the hope of eternal life in Christ Jesus our Lord.

To Him be the glory—now and forever.

Edward D. Andrews

Author of over 220 book and Chief Translator of the Updated American Standard Version

INTRODUCTION

Evangelism stands at the very center of the Christian faith. It is not an optional pursuit for the spiritually elite but a divine command given to all who have been reconciled to God through Jesus Christ. The Great Commission—to go and make disciples of all nations (Matthew 28:19–20)—is the heartbeat of Scripture and the enduring mission of the Church. Yet, in every generation, believers must rediscover what it means to proclaim the gospel with clarity, conviction, and compassion. *Reasoning from the Scriptures* seeks to do precisely that: to call Christians back to the biblical model of evangelism grounded in truth and guided by love.

The phrase "reasoning from the Scriptures," drawn from the book of Acts, describes the apostolic approach to evangelism. When Paul entered the synagogues, he did not appeal to emotion, social reform, or human philosophy. Luke records, "He reasoned with them from the Scriptures, explaining and giving evidence that the Christ had to suffer and rise again from the dead, and saying, 'This Jesus whom I am proclaiming to you is the Christ'" (Acts 17:2–3). That passage defines the essence of authentic evangelism—proclaiming divine truth through sound reasoning, clear explanation, and persuasive conviction.

The early Christians changed the world not through cultural influence, wealth, or political power, but through the transforming power of God's Word. Their message was simple yet profound: salvation through the death and resurrection of Jesus Christ. Their authority was not their personality or education, but the inspired Scriptures that testified to Christ. Their method was reasoning, explaining, proving, and persuading; their motive was love for God and compassion for lost souls. This same pattern must define evangelism today.

In a modern world dominated by skepticism, relativism, and distraction, Christians face challenges that mirror those of the first century. Many reject the Bible as irrelevant or untrustworthy. Others embrace the idea that all religions lead to the same destination. Still others, though spiritually hungry, wander aimlessly amid a flood of false philosophies. In such an environment, the need for believers who can *reason from the Scriptures*—anchored in truth, equipped with understanding, and filled with grace—is more urgent than ever.

This book is designed to equip every Christian, from new believers to seasoned servants of God, to share the gospel effectively in an age of confusion. Each chapter explores a specific aspect of evangelism—how to understand your audience, how to overcome fear, how to present the message of salvation, and how to answer common objections with gentleness and reverence. The book also examines the examples of Jesus Christ and the Apostle Paul, demonstrating how both combined spiritual wisdom with persuasive communication to reach hearts and minds.

The goal of this work is not merely to provide information but to inspire transformation. Evangelism must flow from a life shaped by truth and holiness. To proclaim Christ effectively, one must know Him deeply. The most powerful witness is not found in eloquent speech but in the consistent testimony of a life governed by Scripture. The gospel cannot be separated from the character of the one who proclaims it. As Paul reminded the Thessalonians, "Our gospel did not come to you in word only, but also in power and in the Holy Spirit and with full conviction" (1 Thessalonians 1:5).

To reason from the Scriptures is to restore confidence in the power of God's Word. The Bible remains the ultimate authority for faith and life. It is the sword of the Spirit (Ephesians 6:17), sharper than any human argument, and able to pierce the conscience and awaken repentance. Human reasoning alone cannot change the heart, but when aligned with divine truth, it becomes a powerful instrument in the hands of the faithful.

Throughout the pages of this book, you will encounter both theological insight and practical application. You will learn how to engage skeptics with logic and humility, how to approach seekers with patience and understanding, and how to communicate biblical truth in ways that reach the intellect and the heart alike. Each chapter is rooted in Scripture, applying its timeless wisdom to the realities of our present world.

The task before us is immense, but the promise of God is sure. The gospel remains "the power of God for salvation to everyone who believes" (Romans 1:16). The message has not changed, and neither has its power. The same Word that turned idol-worshipers into worshipers of Christ in the first century can still bring light to darkened minds today.

Reasoning from the Scriptures calls believers to return to the apostolic pattern—reasoning with clarity, explaining with accuracy, proving with evidence, and persuading with love. It challenges every Christian to rise above fear, apathy, and indifference, and to embrace the high calling of being Christ's witnesses in a world desperate for truth.

May this book strengthen your faith, sharpen your understanding, and ignite your passion for evangelism. May it remind you that every conversation is a divine appointment, every question an opportunity, and every soul a treasure of infinite worth in the eyes of God.

And may you, like Paul, be able to say with joy and conviction, "I did not shrink from declaring to you the whole purpose of God" (Acts 20:27).

CHAPTER 1 Evangelism: The Divine Mandate to Proclaim the Good News

Evangelism stands at the very heart of Christianity. It is not a mere program, occasional outreach, or optional expression of faith, but the central commission of the Church and the divine responsibility of every believer. From the moment Jesus Christ declared, "Go therefore and make disciples of all the nations" (Matthew 28:19), the task of evangelism was embedded into the life and mission of the body of Christ. The act of evangelism is both the proclamation and the embodiment of the message of salvation—announcing the good news that through Jesus Christ, Jehovah has provided redemption from sin, reconciliation with Himself, and the hope of eternal life.

The Biblical Foundation of Evangelism

The foundation of evangelism rests entirely upon the authority and example of Jesus Christ. He came to seek and to save that which was lost (Luke 19:10), and He passed that same purpose to His followers. The

Greek term *euangelion* (translated "gospel" or "good news") literally means "a message of victory" or "glad tidings." The apostles and early disciples carried this message as heralds of the King, announcing that through Jesus Christ's death and resurrection, mankind could now be reconciled to God.

Evangelism is not a human invention but a divine command. In Matthew 28:18–20, known as the Great Commission, Jesus gave His disciples a universal mandate grounded in His divine authority: "All authority has been given to Me in heaven and on earth." Evangelism therefore flows from Christ's sovereignty and is accomplished under His power. The message is not our own; it is Jehovah's redemptive truth entrusted to faithful men and women to proclaim to a perishing world.

This same commission appears throughout Scripture. In Mark 16:15, Jesus commanded, "Go into all the world and preach the gospel to all creation." In Luke 24:46–48, He said that "repentance for forgiveness of sins should be proclaimed in His name to all the nations." In John 20:21, He stated, "As the Father has sent Me, I also send you." Acts 1:8 provides the model: "You shall receive power when the Holy Spirit has come upon you; and you shall be My witnesses both in Jerusalem, and in all Judea and Samaria, and even to the remotest part of the earth."

The book of Acts records the fulfillment of these words. The disciples, empowered by the Spirit through the Word, boldly declared the gospel in Jerusalem and beyond, despite persecution, imprisonment, and death. Their courage and faithfulness formed the model for all future evangelism—faithful proclamation, regardless of the cost.

The Message of Evangelism

The core message of evangelism is not social reform, emotional experience, or moral improvement, but the truth of salvation through Jesus Christ. Paul summarized this gospel clearly in 1 Corinthians 15:3–4: "That Christ died for our sins according to the Scriptures, and that He was buried, and that He was raised on the third day according to the Scriptures." This is the unchanging foundation of all evangelism—the substitutionary death and bodily resurrection of Jesus Christ for the forgiveness of sins.

Humanity is utterly lost apart from Christ. Romans 3:23 declares, "All have sinned and fall short of the glory of God." Sin separates man from Jehovah, and no human effort, ritual, or moral striving can remove that guilt. The penalty of sin is death—cessation of life, the end of personhood, and eternal destruction in Gehenna for the unrepentant (Romans

6:23). Yet Jehovah, out of His love, sent His Son to bear that penalty in our place. Through faith and repentance, individuals are justified, forgiven, and reconciled to God.

Evangelism, therefore, centers on repentance and faith. Jesus began His ministry with the call, "Repent, for the kingdom of heaven is at hand" (Matthew 4:17). Faith is not mere intellectual assent, but active trust and commitment to Christ as Lord and Savior. Evangelism must clearly proclaim both: turning from sin and turning to God through Christ. Any message that neglects repentance, the cross, or the exclusivity of Christ is not the biblical gospel.

The Responsibility of Every Believer

Evangelism is not limited to clergy, missionaries, or church leaders. It is the calling of every believer who has experienced the saving grace of God. The early Church was not advanced by professional evangelists, but by ordinary Christians who spoke the Word wherever they went (Acts 8:4).

In 2 Corinthians 5:18–20, Paul describes believers as ambassadors for Christ, entrusted with the ministry of reconciliation. This term conveys both authority and responsibility—believers represent the

King and speak on His behalf, calling others to be reconciled to Him. Evangelism is therefore not optional; it is the natural expression of a transformed life and the central purpose of Christian existence.

Every Christian is to be ready "to make a defense to everyone who asks you to give an account for the hope that is in you" (1 Peter 3:15). This readiness involves knowing Scripture, understanding the message of salvation, and being prepared to communicate it clearly and lovingly. Evangelism is not about clever argumentation or manipulation, but faithfully presenting the truth and trusting Jehovah to convict and convert.

The Method of Evangelism

The biblical method of evangelism involves both verbal proclamation and godly living. The gospel must be spoken, for "faith comes from hearing, and hearing by the word of Christ" (Romans 10:17). Yet the messenger's conduct must also reflect the message, for hypocrisy undermines credibility. The most effective evangelism combines sound doctrine with genuine character.

Jesus modeled personal engagement with individuals—the Samaritan woman at the well (John 4), Nicodemus (John 3), Zacchaeus (Luke 19)—

demonstrating that evangelism is both personal and relational. He met people where they were, addressed their spiritual needs, and directed them toward repentance and faith. Likewise, believers today must engage others with compassion, patience, and truth, never compromising the message to gain acceptance.

Public preaching also has its place, as seen in Peter's sermon at Pentecost (Acts 2) and Paul's address in Athens (Acts 17). Whether in the marketplace, the home, or the assembly, the gospel must be proclaimed without dilution or apology. The central focus must remain the person and work of Christ, not entertainment, emotionalism, or worldly persuasion.

The Power Behind Evangelism

True evangelism is accomplished not by human skill, charisma, or strategy, but by the power of the Spirit through the Word of God. The Holy Spirit, Who inspired the Scriptures, operates through that Word to convict hearts, illuminate truth, and draw individuals to repentance. It is Jehovah Who saves; evangelists are merely instruments. Paul wrote, "I planted, Apollos watered, but God was causing the growth" (1 Corinthians 3:6).

Therefore, the success of evangelism is not measured by numbers, but by faithfulness to the message. Many rejected Christ Himself, and many will reject His messengers. Yet the evangelist's duty remains the same—to proclaim the truth in love, leaving the results to God.

The Urgency of Evangelism

Evangelism carries an eternal urgency. Every human being faces one of two destinies: eternal life in God's Kingdom or eternal destruction in Gehenna. The brevity of life and the reality of judgment demand that the gospel be proclaimed now. Jesus declared, "We must work the works of Him who sent Me as long as it is day; night is coming when no one can work" (John 9:4).

The apostle Paul expressed this urgency in Romans 10:13–15: "Whoever will call on the name of the Lord will be saved. How then will they call on Him in whom they have not believed? ... And how will they hear without a preacher?" The logic is undeniable: the world cannot believe what it has not heard, and it cannot hear unless believers proclaim the truth. Silence in the face of perishing souls is disobedience to Christ and disregard for His compassion.

The Rewards and Joy of Evangelism

Evangelism is both a duty and a privilege. Those who faithfully share the gospel participate in the greatest work in the universe—the redemption of souls. The joy that accompanies seeing someone come to repentance and faith is indescribable. Paul called the believers in Thessalonica his "hope, joy, and crown of exultation" (1 Thessalonians 2:19).

Beyond temporal joy, there is eternal reward. Daniel 12:3 states, "Those who lead the many to righteousness will shine like the stars forever and ever." Every act of faithful witness, whether seen or unseen, contributes to the eternal glory of God's Kingdom. Evangelism, therefore, is not a burden but a blessing—an expression of gratitude for the salvation we have received and a participation in God's redemptive plan.

The Enduring Mission of the Church

Until Christ returns, the Church's central mission remains unchanged: proclaiming the gospel to all nations, baptizing new believers, and teaching them to obey all that Christ commanded (Matthew 28:19–20). Evangelism fuels discipleship, church growth, and global missions. The Church that ceases to evangelize forfeits its reason for existence.

Every generation of believers stands as a link in the chain of gospel proclamation stretching from the apostles to the end of the age. Each Christian carries the responsibility to preserve and pass on the message of salvation without alteration or compromise. The world's darkness grows deeper, but the light of the gospel shines ever brighter through faithful witnesses who speak truth with courage and compassion.

Conclusion

Evangelism is not merely one aspect of Christian life—it is the heartbeat of Christianity itself. It reflects the love of Jehovah, the sacrifice of Christ, and the mission of the Church. Every believer, empowered by the truth of Scripture, must take up this divine commission with boldness, humility, and unwavering faith. Through evangelism, Jehovah continues His work of calling people out of darkness into His marvelous light.

CHAPTER 2 Evangelism: Proclaiming the Kingdom of God in a World of Darkness

Evangelism is the heartbeat of the Christian faith and the divine instrument by which Jehovah draws humanity out of darkness into the light of His truth. From Genesis to Revelation, Scripture reveals a consistent pattern—Jehovah has always desired that His truth be known among all peoples. Evangelism, therefore, is not simply an activity of the Church but the very expression of God's redemptive will. Through the message of the gospel, He extends the offer of salvation to all who will believe in His Son, Jesus Christ.

The Divine Nature of Evangelism

Evangelism originates with Jehovah Himself. He is the first Evangelist. From the moment Adam and Eve sinned, Jehovah announced the promise of redemption through the Seed who would crush the serpent's head (Genesis 3:15). Throughout history, He has revealed His plan through patriarchs, prophets, and ultimately through His Son. Jesus

Christ embodied the good news—He was both the Messenger and the Message.

When Jesus began His public ministry, He declared, "The time is fulfilled, and the kingdom of God is at hand; repent and believe in the gospel" (Mark 1:15). This statement summarized the essence of all evangelism: the announcement that Jehovah's Kingdom is near, the call to repentance, and the invitation to faith. Evangelism is not an invention of man, nor is it driven by organizational agendas. It is a divine calling and a sacred trust, originating in the heart of God and accomplished through His Word.

The Gospel Message Defined

True evangelism must always center on the message of salvation through Christ. The word *gospel* (*euangelion*) means "good news," but its content must be biblically defined, not culturally shaped. The good news is not that God wants to improve human circumstances or fulfill personal desires, but that He has provided a way to rescue mankind from sin and death.

Paul defined this gospel clearly in Romans 1:16–17: "For I am not ashamed of the gospel, for it is the power of God for salvation to everyone who believes... for in it the righteousness of God is revealed from faith to faith." The gospel is the divine power that delivers sinners from condemnation and grants them eternal life through faith in Christ.

Humanity's need for this message is universal. Scripture teaches that all have sinned (Romans 3:23), that the heart is deceitful above all things (Jeremiah 17:9), and that sin results in death (Romans 6:23). Man, left to himself, has no hope of salvation. Evangelism announces Jehovah's solution: "Christ Jesus came into the world to save sinners" (1 Timothy 1:15).

Through His sacrificial death, Jesus bore the penalty of sin on behalf of humanity. Through His resurrection, He conquered death and opened the way to life. The gospel calls all people to respond through repentance—turning away from sin—and faith—trusting completely in Christ for salvation. This dual call is essential to true evangelism. Without repentance and faith, no one can be saved, regardless of religious activity or moral behavior.

Evangelism in the Ministry of Jesus

Jesus' entire earthly ministry was one of evangelism. He went from village to village preaching the good news of the Kingdom (Luke 8:1). He healed the sick, cast out demons, and performed miracles, but these acts were never ends in themselves—they confirmed the message of salvation. He came not to entertain crowds or improve society, but to call sinners to repentance (Luke 5:32).

Jesus' method of evangelism combined public proclamation with personal conversation. He preached to multitudes, but He also engaged individuals—the Samaritan woman, Nicodemus, the rich young ruler. His approach was relational yet uncompromising, compassionate yet confrontational when necessary. He never softened the truth to gain followers. When many turned away because of His hard sayings, He did not alter His message to keep them (John 6:66–67).

This model defines biblical evangelism. It is neither harsh nor sentimental, neither intellectualism nor emotional manipulation. It is the clear, authoritative declaration of Jehovah's truth in love, calling people to repentance and faith.

The Apostolic Continuation

After His resurrection, Jesus commissioned His followers to continue the work He began. He said, "Go therefore and make disciples of all the nations" (Matthew 28:19). The command was not to merely make converts, but to make disciples—men and women who would be taught to observe all that Christ commanded.

The book of Acts records how the early believers fulfilled this command. Empowered by the Word and driven by conviction, they proclaimed the gospel everywhere. Peter preached at Pentecost, declaring Jesus as both Lord and Christ. Thousands were cut to the heart and repented. Stephen testified boldly before his executioners. Philip preached to the Ethiopian eunuch. Paul carried the message to Jews and Gentiles alike across the Roman Empire.

The early Church grew not through marketing or political power, but through the unrelenting proclamation of truth. They faced persecution, imprisonment, and death, yet the gospel spread because it was the power of God, not the work of man. Their obedience established a pattern for all believers throughout history—the gospel must go forth regardless of the cost.

The Theology of Evangelism

Theologically, evangelism rests on several unchangeable truths. First, Jehovah is sovereign in salvation. He calls and draws people through His Word. Second, Jesus Christ is the only means of salvation. Acts 4:12 declares, "There is salvation in no one else." Third, the message of the gospel is unalterable; it cannot be improved, diluted, or contextualized to fit modern preferences. Fourth, the responsibility of proclamation belongs to every believer.

Evangelism is not about results or numbers but faithfulness. Paul wrote, "We speak, not as pleasing men, but God who examines our hearts" (1 Thessalonians 2:4). Success in evangelism is measured not by the response of others, but by the obedience of the messenger. The gospel is a seed that Jehovah causes to grow in His timing and according to His purpose.

The Means and Methods of Evangelism

While the message never changes, the means of communication may vary according to time and culture. Yet even here, the Church must be careful. Evangelism must remain centered on Scripture and truth, not entertainment or worldly appeal. Modern trends that substitute music, spectacle, or emotional manipulation for clear gospel teaching have abandoned the biblical model.

True evangelism depends upon the proclamation of the Word of God. Romans 10:17 states, "Faith comes from hearing, and hearing by the word of Christ." This truth demands that evangelists know Scripture, explain it faithfully, and apply it clearly. The power is not in the personality of the speaker, but in the authority of the message.

Personal evangelism also remains vital. Every believer encounters people daily who may never enter a church building. Family members, co-workers, and neighbors represent mission fields in themselves. A Christian's conduct, speech, and compassion should reflect Christ and open doors for witness. However, lifestyle alone is insufficient; the gospel must be spoken. Without the clear communication of Christ's atoning work, there is no evangelism.

The Role of the Church

The local congregation serves as the base of evangelistic activity. Through the Church, believers are equipped, trained, and encouraged to proclaim the gospel. Ephesians 4:11–12 states that Christ gave apostles, prophets, evangelists, pastors, and teachers "for the equipping of the holy ones for the work of service." The primary responsibility of leadership is to prepare believers for evangelism and discipleship, not to entertain them or provide social programs.

Corporate evangelism includes public preaching, community outreach, and missions. Yet every organized effort must remain faithful to the content of Scripture. The Church must avoid reducing the gospel to a message of self-improvement, prosperity, or social justice. Evangelism is about reconciliation between God and man, not about solving temporal problems.

The Obstacles to Evangelism

Throughout history, evangelism has faced opposition from the world, from false religion, and from human apathy. Satan, as the god of this age, blinds the minds of unbelievers (2 Corinthians 4:4). False teachers distort the gospel, adding works, traditions, or mysticism. The world ridicules the message as foolishness (1 Corinthians 1:18). Even within the Church, fear, complacency, and compromise hinder evangelism.

Yet Jehovah's Word promises that His message will not return empty (Isaiah 55:11). The light of truth cannot be extinguished by darkness. Every generation of believers must overcome these obstacles by standing firm on Scripture and boldly proclaiming Christ.

The Urgency and Compassion of Evangelism

Evangelism is urgent because eternity hangs in the balance. Each day countless souls pass into gravedom without hope. The reality of judgment should stir the hearts of believers to compassion. Jesus wept over Jerusalem, saying, "If you had known... the things which make for peace!" (Luke 19:42). Likewise, those who know the gospel should be moved by love to share it.

Paul declared, "Woe is me if I do not preach the gospel!" (1 Corinthians 9:16). Such passion arises from gratitude for one's own salvation and concern for others' eternal destiny. Evangelism must never become mechanical or prideful; it is an act of love that mirrors the compassion of Christ.

The Eternal Impact of Evangelism

Every act of evangelism echoes into eternity. Those who respond in faith are transferred from death to life, from darkness to light. Their transformation glorifies Jehovah and fulfills His eternal purpose in Christ. The evangelist shares in that joy.

Scripture speaks of the eternal reward for those who labor faithfully. Paul told the Philippians that they were his "joy and crown" (Philippians 4:1). Daniel 12:3 describes those who lead many to righteousness as shining "like the stars forever." Evangelism thus carries both present and eternal significance—it honors God now and secures everlasting joy in His Kingdom.

The Consummation of Evangelism

The mission of evangelism will continue until Christ returns. In Matthew 24:14, Jesus declared, "This gospel of the kingdom shall be preached in the whole world as a testimony to all the nations, and then the end will come." The completion of global evangelization is directly tied to the consummation of God's plan. Until that day, the Church must remain steadfast in its witness.

The gospel began in Jerusalem, spread to Judea, Samaria, and the ends of the earth. It continues today through faithful believers who proclaim Christ's name amid opposition. Each redeemed soul becomes another witness, another light in the world, another voice proclaiming that Jehovah saves.

Evangelism is not merely about filling churches; it is about populating eternity with those reconciled to God. The task is immense, but the authority and power belong to Christ. He promised, "I am with you always, even to the end of the age" (Matthew 28:20).

CHAPTER 3 The Art of Evangelism: Proclaiming Truth with Wisdom, Courage, and Compassion

Evangelism is not merely a duty but a sacred art—the divinely ordained craft of communicating eternal truth to fallen humanity. It requires knowledge, discernment, sincerity, and spiritual courage. The art of evangelism is the deliberate and skillful expression of Jehovah's saving message through the believer's words, character, and conduct. It reflects both the majesty of God's truth and the compassion of His heart toward the lost. While the gospel itself is unchanging, the way in which it is presented—its clarity, tone, and manner—must display the wisdom and grace of the One Who commissioned it.

The Divine Origin and Purpose of Evangelism

Evangelism originates from Jehovah's eternal purpose to redeem mankind through Jesus Christ. Before the foundation of the world, God's redemptive plan was established (Ephesians 1:4–5). The Son of God came "to seek and to save that which was lost"

(Luke 19:10), and He has entrusted this same mission to His followers. The believer's responsibility is not to innovate a message but to faithfully declare what has already been revealed.

The purpose of evangelism is twofold: to glorify Jehovah and to reconcile sinners to Him. Evangelism is not primarily about human satisfaction or religious experience but about the exaltation of God's holiness and mercy through the proclamation of truth. As Paul wrote, "We are ambassadors for Christ, as though God were making an appeal through us" (2 Corinthians 5:20). The art of evangelism, therefore, lies in representing the King faithfully and communicating His message accurately, with reverence and humility.

Evangelism as an Art of Divine Communication

The art of evangelism is rooted in divine communication. Jehovah has revealed Himself through creation, conscience, Scripture, and ultimately through Christ. Evangelism continues that revelation by explaining and applying it to the hearts of men. The evangelist becomes a vessel through whom God's truth is spoken with clarity and conviction.

The effectiveness of evangelism depends not on human eloquence but on the faithfulness of the message and the purity of the messenger. Paul deliberately avoided "persuasive words of wisdom" so that the faith of his hearers would rest not on human skill but on the power of God (1 Corinthians 2:4–5). Yet Paul was also intentional, thoughtful, and strategic in how he presented the gospel—reasoning in synagogues, appealing to the conscience of Gentiles, and adapting his approach without compromising truth.

Thus, the art of evangelism is both divine and human. It is divine in origin and message but human in delivery. It requires understanding people's minds, addressing their needs, and guiding them to the truth with patience and wisdom. The evangelist must speak truth that pierces the conscience, yet do so with a heart that reflects Christ's compassion.

The Message: The Unchanging Core of Evangelism

At the heart of all true evangelism lies one message—the gospel of Jesus Christ. Paul summarized it succinctly: "That Christ died for our sins according to the Scriptures, and that He was buried, and that He was raised on the third day" (1 Corinthians 15:3–4). This message cannot be improved, updated, or softened. It remains eternally relevant because the problem of sin remains unchanged.

Evangelism must declare that all humans are sinners separated from Jehovah, deserving of death, and incapable of saving themselves. It must proclaim that Jesus Christ alone, through His sacrificial death and resurrection, provides the means of reconciliation. The gospel demands repentance—turning from sin—and faith—complete trust in Christ's atoning work. Anything less is not biblical evangelism but spiritual deception.

The art of evangelism therefore does not lie in creativity of content but in faithfulness of communication. The evangelist's task is to present this truth in a way that confronts sin, clarifies grace, and calls for decision, without diluting or distorting the message.

The Heart of the Evangelist

Evangelism is not merely an act of speech but an overflow of the heart. A genuine evangelist is one whose soul burns with gratitude for personal salvation and compassion for the lost. When Jesus looked upon the crowds, He "felt compassion for them, because they were distressed and dispirited like sheep without a shepherd" (Matthew 9:36). This divine compassion drove His ministry and must likewise drive ours.

The heart of the evangelist must be humble before God and tender toward people. Pride, impatience, or anger have no place in gospel proclamation. The message must be presented in love, not arrogance. Paul reminded Timothy, "The Lord's bond-servant must not be quarrelsome, but be kind to all, able to teach, patient when wronged, with gentleness correcting those who are in opposition" (2 Timothy 2:24–25).

The art of evangelism, therefore, is inseparable from the character of the evangelist. Words spoken without love or holiness lose their power. The purity of one's life validates the truth of one's message. A godly example adorns the gospel; hypocrisy discredits it.

The Art of Listening and Understanding

Evangelism is not a one-sided monologue but a conversation that requires discernment and empathy. Jesus listened before He spoke. When He met the Samaritan woman at the well (John 4), He began by engaging her in ordinary dialogue, then gradually directed the conversation toward her deepest spiritual need. He understood her heart and used her own words to reveal truth.

The art of evangelism involves perceiving the obstacles in another person's heart—ignorance, pride, fear, or false belief—and addressing them wisely with Scripture. Paul exemplified this when he preached in Athens (Acts 17). He began with the Athenians' own religious curiosity, then redirected their thoughts to the true and living God. He did not begin by condemning but by revealing. Yet he did not end with compromise—he called them to repentance.

Effective evangelists understand both the message and the audience. They study Scripture deeply and observe the culture carefully, discerning how best to communicate truth without surrendering it.

The Role of Scripture in Evangelism

Scripture is the soul of evangelism. The Word of God alone possesses the power to convict, enlighten, and transform. Human reasoning, emotion, or testimony may assist, but only the Scriptures carry divine authority. Hebrews 4:12 declares, "The word of God is living and active and sharper than any two-edged sword."

The art of evangelism depends on skillful use of Scripture. The evangelist must know the Word thoroughly—its doctrines, promises, and commands—and be ready to apply it in every circumstance. Jesus Himself modeled this in His evangelistic conversations, constantly quoting or alluding to Scripture. When He explained His identity to the disciples on the road to Emmaus, He began "with Moses and with all the prophets" (Luke 24:27).

The evangelist should therefore be a student of the Bible, able to explain salvation clearly and answer objections with gentleness and confidence. Evangelism without Scripture is powerless persuasion; evangelism with Scripture is divine truth unleashed.

The Balance of Boldness and Gentleness

The art of evangelism requires both boldness and gentleness. Boldness without gentleness becomes harshness; gentleness without boldness becomes weakness. True biblical evangelism reflects both the authority of truth and the tenderness of grace.

The apostles spoke with great courage, declaring that "we cannot stop speaking about what we have seen and heard" (Acts 4:20). Their boldness was not arrogance but conviction born from the assurance that their message came from God. They feared Jehovah more than men.

At the same time, they demonstrated deep humility and compassion. Paul reminded the Thessalonians that he had been "gentle among you, as a nursing mother tenderly cares for her own children" (1 Thessalonians 2:7). This combination of courage and compassion defines the art of evangelism. The truth must be declared fearlessly, yet always with the goal of winning souls, not arguments.

The Discipline of Prayer in Evangelism

Prayer is essential to the art of evangelism. The evangelist must pray for wisdom, guidance, and divine opportunity. Jesus instructed His disciples, "The harvest is plentiful, but the workers are few. Therefore beseech the Lord of the harvest to send out workers into His harvest" (Matthew 9:37–38).

Prayer prepares both the messenger and the hearer. It humbles the evangelist, reminding him that conversion is God's work, not human achievement. It softens the hearts of those who will hear, opening them to receive truth. Paul constantly requested prayer from fellow believers, that "God will open up to us a door for the word" (Colossians 4:3).

Evangelism without prayer becomes mechanical and fruitless; evangelism rooted in prayer becomes powerful and effective. The art of evangelism thrives in dependence upon Jehovah's grace.

The Role of the Local Church

The art of evangelism is cultivated and supported within the local congregation. The Church is the training ground where believers learn to share their faith, grow in knowledge, and practice obedience. Evangelism is not an isolated act but a collective mission of the body of Christ.

Church leaders must equip believers for evangelistic ministry (Ephesians 4:11–12). This includes teaching sound doctrine, modeling compassion for the lost, and encouraging personal witness. Congregations that focus inwardly soon stagnate; those that prioritize evangelism experience spiritual vitality.

The Church also provides accountability and fellowship for evangelists. Those who labor to spread the gospel need encouragement, prayer, and partnership. The early believers in Acts exemplified this unity—they prayed together, preached together, and rejoiced together when souls were saved.

The Art of Perseverance

Evangelism requires perseverance. Many will reject the message, mock the messenger, or remain indifferent. Yet the evangelist must remain steadfast, knowing that his labor is never in vain. Jesus warned that the world would hate those who follow Him (John 15:18–20). Paul endured persecution, imprisonment, and hardship but never ceased proclaiming Christ.

The art of evangelism includes the discipline of endurance—the ability to continue faithfully even when results seem invisible. Jehovah measures success by faithfulness, not popularity. The evangelist sows the seed; God gives the growth.

The Eternal Fruit of Evangelism

The art of evangelism produces eternal fruit. Every soul that responds to the gospel glorifies Jehovah and adds to the number of those redeemed by the Lamb. The joy of leading another person to salvation surpasses any earthly achievement. The evangelist participates in the fulfillment of God's eternal plan and shares in the joy of Heaven itself.

Jesus declared, "There is joy in the presence of the angels of God over one sinner who repents" (Luke 15:10). That joy becomes the evangelist's reward. Daniel 12:3 promises, "Those who have insight will shine brightly like the brightness of the expanse of heaven, and those who lead the many to righteousness, like the stars forever and ever."

Evangelism, therefore, is the highest art—a sacred craft that combines divine truth, spiritual wisdom, and compassionate love. It is the means by which Jehovah calls the lost to life, the Church fulfills its mission, and the believer honors his Redeemer.

CHAPTER 4 The Role of Scripture in Evangelism: The Power of God's Word to Convict, Convert, and Transform

Evangelism is the divinely appointed means by which Jehovah's truth is proclaimed to a lost and dying world. Yet the true power behind all evangelistic work does not lie in human eloquence, persuasive speech, or emotional appeal, but in the living Word of God. Scripture is not a mere aid to evangelism; it is the very essence and authority of it. Without Scripture, evangelism loses its foundation, message, and effectiveness. The Word of God is the instrument through which Jehovah reveals His will, exposes sin, convicts the heart, and brings about genuine faith. Therefore, understanding the role of Scripture in evangelism is essential to understanding the nature and success of evangelism itself.

The Divine Origin of Scripture

Scripture is not a human product but divine revelation. Paul wrote, "All Scripture is inspired by

God and profitable for teaching, for reproof, for correction, for training in righteousness" (2 Timothy 3:16). The term "inspired" (Greek *theopneustos*) means "God-breathed." Thus, every word of Scripture originates from Jehovah Himself. Evangelism therefore begins with confidence in the absolute authority, inerrancy, and sufficiency of the Bible.

Because Scripture is God's Word, it possesses inherent power. Unlike human opinion, it does not depend on the skill of the messenger or the openness of the listener. Jehovah declared through Isaiah, "So will My word be which goes forth from My mouth; it will not return to Me empty, without accomplishing what I desire" (Isaiah 55:11). The Word accomplishes God's purpose because it carries His divine authority. It pierces, judges, and transforms the human heart.

The evangelist must therefore trust wholly in Scripture. No method, technique, or philosophy can substitute for the Spirit-inspired Word. The art of evangelism begins not with innovation, but with submission—to the authority of Scripture as the exclusive source of truth and the sole message of salvation.

The Word of God as the Foundation of Evangelism

The entire mission of evangelism rests upon Scripture, for it reveals the gospel itself. Without the Bible, humanity would have no knowledge of Jehovah's character, sin's seriousness, or Christ's redemptive work. Paul affirmed that "faith comes from hearing, and hearing by the word of Christ" (Romans 10:17). Evangelism apart from Scripture cannot produce genuine faith because true faith is a response to divine revelation.

The gospel message is not the invention of man but the declaration of Scripture: "That Christ died for our sins according to the Scriptures, and that He was buried, and that He was raised on the third day according to the Scriptures" (1 Corinthians 15:3–4). The authority of evangelism, therefore, rests not in the evangelist but in the Scriptures he proclaims. The evangelist is merely a herald of divine truth, commissioned to speak what has already been spoken by God.

When the early Christians evangelized, they consistently relied upon the Scriptures. Peter's sermon at Pentecost (Acts 2) was a thorough exposition of the Old Testament, showing that Jesus fulfilled prophecy. Stephen's defense before the

Sanhedrin (Acts 7) traced God's redemptive history through Scripture. Philip explained Isaiah 53 to the Ethiopian eunuch and then proclaimed Jesus as the suffering Servant (Acts 8:30–35). Paul, wherever he went, "reasoned with them from the Scriptures" (Acts 17:2). Every example in the New Testament demonstrates that evangelism depends entirely on the Word of God.

Scripture as the Revealer of Sin and Human Need

Before anyone can embrace the gospel, he must first understand his need for it. Scripture performs this essential function by revealing sin in its true light. Paul wrote, "Through the Law comes the knowledge of sin" (Romans 3:20). The Bible exposes the moral failure of mankind, showing that all have sinned and stand guilty before Jehovah (Romans 3:23).

Evangelism that neglects Scripture cannot produce genuine conviction of sin. Only the Word of God can expose the heart's corruption, revealing the depth of humanity's alienation from God. Hebrews 4:12 declares, "The word of God is living and active and sharper than any two-edged sword, and piercing as far as the division of soul and spirit… and able to judge the thoughts and intentions of the heart." The evangelist does not need to manipulate emotions or create artificial guilt; Scripture itself penetrates to the conscience, laying bare the truth.

When Nathan confronted David after his sin with Bathsheba, he did not rely on personal rebuke but on divine revelation: "You are the man!" (2 Samuel 12:7). That single prophetic declaration, grounded in God's Word, brought the king to repentance. Likewise, Scripture remains the divine tool through which sinners are convicted of sin and drawn to repentance.

Scripture as the Revelation of Salvation

While Scripture exposes sin, it also reveals the only solution—salvation through Jesus Christ. The Word of God unfolds the entire plan of redemption: Jehovah's holiness, man's fall, Christ's substitutionary sacrifice, and the promise of eternal life through faith. Without Scripture, none of this could be known.

Evangelism must therefore present the gospel exactly as Scripture defines it. Any message that omits sin, repentance, the cross, or the resurrection ceases to be biblical evangelism. Jesus Himself used Scripture to explain salvation. On the road to Emmaus, He "explained to them the things concerning Himself in all the Scriptures" (Luke 24:27). The apostles did the same, showing from the Scriptures that Jesus was the Messiah who fulfilled prophecy.

The Word of God is not only the content of evangelism but also the means of regeneration. Peter wrote, "You have been born again not of seed which is perishable but imperishable, that is, through the living and enduring word of God" (1 Peter 1:23). The Word is the seed that brings forth new spiritual life. When it is faithfully proclaimed, Jehovah Himself works through it to awaken faith and produce repentance.

Scripture and the Power to Convict and Convert

The role of Scripture in evangelism extends beyond revelation; it is the divine instrument of conviction and conversion. The Holy Spirit works exclusively through the Word He inspired, using it to awaken the conscience, enlighten the mind, and transform the heart.

When Peter preached at Pentecost, his message consisted almost entirely of Scripture. The result was not mere intellectual agreement but deep conviction: "When they heard this, they were pierced to the heart" (Acts 2:37). This piercing was not caused by Peter's passion or eloquence, but by the power of the Word he proclaimed.

Likewise, Paul reminded the Thessalonians that "our gospel did not come to you in word only, but also in power and in the Holy Spirit" (1 Thessalonians 1:5). The Spirit and the Word always work together. The Spirit does not bypass the Word to save, nor does the Word work apart from the Spirit. The Holy Spirit operates through Scripture to bring sinners to repentance and faith.

This truth must anchor all evangelistic work. Methods and presentations may vary, but the power to save remains solely in the proclaimed Word. As Paul declared, "The gospel... is the power of God for salvation to everyone who believes" (Romans 1:16).

Scripture as the Standard of Truth in Evangelism

In every generation, false gospels have attempted to distort the message of salvation—whether by adding works, emphasizing emotion, or compromising truth. Scripture serves as the only safeguard against such corruption. It is the divine standard by which every evangelistic message must be tested.

The Bereans were commended for examining "the Scriptures daily to see whether these things were so" (Acts 17:11). True evangelism welcomes such examination, because it rests upon Scripture's unchanging truth. The evangelist who faithfully proclaims the Bible never fears scrutiny; his authority comes not from himself but from the inspired text.

The art of evangelism, therefore, requires scriptural precision. It demands that the gospel be presented as the Bible defines it—neither expanded by human philosophy nor reduced by cultural convenience. The message must remain as unaltered as the Word from which it comes.

Scripture as the Guide for the Evangelist

The role of Scripture in evangelism extends also to the guidance of the evangelist himself. The Bible instructs the believer in how to proclaim truth with wisdom, courage, and compassion. It provides both the message and the manner.

Paul exhorted Timothy, "Preach the word; be ready in season and out of season; reprove, rebuke, exhort, with great patience and instruction" (2 Timothy 4:2). The command to "preach the word" defines the essence of evangelistic duty. The evangelist must be ready at all times, grounded in Scripture, and motivated by obedience rather than circumstance.

Scripture also shapes the character of the evangelist. It teaches humility, holiness, and love. The messenger's life must reflect the truth he proclaims. A contradiction between conduct and message undermines the credibility of the gospel. Thus, evangelism must always be accompanied by a life transformed by Scripture.

The Word of God and the Discipleship That Follows Evangelism

Evangelism does not end with conversion; it continues through discipleship, which is likewise grounded in Scripture. Jesus commanded, "Go therefore and make disciples... teaching them to observe all that I commanded you" (Matthew 28:19–20). The goal of evangelism is not merely to produce converts but to produce obedient followers of Christ who live according to His Word.

The same Scripture that saves also sanctifies. Jesus prayed, "Sanctify them in the truth; Your word is truth" (John 17:17). Through continual study and obedience to Scripture, the new believer grows in faith and maturity. Therefore, evangelism that does not lead to scriptural instruction is incomplete. The role of the Bible in evangelism continues long after initial conversion—it shapes the entire Christian life.

The Sufficiency of Scripture in Evangelism

In an age of religious pluralism, psychological manipulation, and emotional spectacle, it is essential to reaffirm the sufficiency of Scripture in evangelism. The Bible contains everything necessary for the salvation of the soul and the transformation of life. No new revelation, mystical experience, or cultural adaptation can improve upon what Jehovah has already revealed.

The evangelist must resist the temptation to rely on entertainment, worldly persuasion, or emotional appeals. The power of evangelism lies not in the attractiveness of presentation but in the truth of revelation. The gospel, as revealed in Scripture, is fully sufficient to convict, convert, and transform those whom Jehovah calls.

The Eternal Impact of Scripture in Evangelism

The role of Scripture in evangelism extends beyond time. Every verse proclaimed in faith accomplishes eternal results. Jesus declared, "Heaven and earth will pass away, but My words will not pass away" (Matthew 24:35). The gospel message endures forever, and those who believe it receive eternal life.

The evangelist who faithfully preaches Scripture participates in an eternal work. He sows imperishable seed that will bear fruit in Jehovah's Kingdom. The results may not always be visible on earth, but they are recorded in Heaven. The Word that convicts and converts today will one day stand as the standard by which all humanity is judged.

Therefore, the role of Scripture in evangelism is ultimate and unchanging. It is the revelation of truth, the source of conviction, the means of salvation, the guide for discipleship, and the eternal record of Jehovah's redemptive plan. To neglect Scripture in evangelism is to abandon the very power of God unto salvation. To proclaim it faithfully is to stand as a vessel through whom the living Word brings life to those dead in sin.

CHAPTER 5 The Character of the Evangelist: Reflecting Christ in Word, Life, and Witness

Evangelism is not only about proclaiming the message of salvation but also about embodying the truth of that message in one's own life. The evangelist's words are powerful only when accompanied by a life consistent with the gospel. Scripture reveals that Jehovah uses faithful, holy vessels to communicate His truth to others. The evangelist's moral and spiritual character, therefore, is not secondary to his mission—it is central to it. Without godly character, even the most accurate message can lose its credibility. The message of Christ must be carried by those who reflect His likeness in their hearts, words, and actions.

The Importance of Character

The power of evangelism is not found merely in persuasive speech or intellectual argumentation but in the integrity and holiness of the messenger. The early apostles were not eloquent philosophers; they were men transformed by the grace of God. Their effectiveness in evangelism arose from the reality of their conversion and their unwavering devotion to Christ.

Character validates the message. Paul wrote to Timothy, "Pay close attention to yourself and to your teaching; persevere in these things, for as you do this you will ensure salvation both for yourself and for those who hear you" (1 Timothy 4:16). The apostle linked personal integrity with ministerial fruitfulness. A lack of character discredits the gospel, while godliness reinforces it.

The evangelist's life is itself an ongoing testimony. His behavior either opens or closes hearts to the truth. When unbelievers observe holiness, humility, love, and authenticity, they see the transforming power of the gospel on display. Thus, the most persuasive evidence of the message's truth is often the character of the one who proclaims it.

The Character Traits of the Evangelist

Scripture identifies several essential character traits that must define every true evangelist. These traits are not natural virtues but spiritual qualities developed through obedience to God's Word.

The evangelist must be humble before God, compassionate toward others, filled with love for souls, courageous in proclaiming truth, and authentic in conduct. He must also exhibit the fruit of the Spirit—love, joy, peace, patience, kindness, goodness, faithfulness, gentleness, and self-control (Galatians 5:22–23). These are not optional virtues but necessary evidences of a life governed by Scripture.

An evangelist who proclaims Christ without reflecting His character contradicts his own message. The gospel calls sinners to transformation, and the evangelist must exemplify that transformation in every area of life.

Cultivating the Character of the Evangelist

The character of the evangelist is not developed through human willpower but through spiritual discipline and dependence upon Jehovah. Paul urged believers, "Discipline yourself for the purpose of godliness" (1 Timothy 4:7). Spiritual character grows through daily submission to the Word of God, prayer, self-examination, and obedience.

Cultivation of godly character begins in the heart. Outward conduct flows from inward conviction. Jesus taught, "The good man out of the good treasure of his heart brings forth what is good" (Luke 6:45). The evangelist must continually guard his heart, for from it flow the issues of life (Proverbs 4:23).

Regular study of Scripture shapes moral conviction and corrects sinful tendencies. Prayer cultivates humility and dependence upon God's grace. Fellowship with mature believers sharpens accountability and strengthens perseverance. Trials refine character, revealing whether faith is genuine. Through all these means, the evangelist learns to reflect Christ more faithfully.

The Need for a Christ-Like Character

The ultimate model for every evangelist is Jesus Christ Himself. He is the perfect example of holiness, compassion, courage, and truth. His earthly ministry demonstrated the character that must define every messenger of the gospel.

Jesus proclaimed the Kingdom of God with unwavering boldness, yet His heart overflowed with mercy toward sinners. He was sinless, yet He associated with the broken and the despised. His humility was profound—though equal with God, He "emptied Himself, taking the form of a bond-servant" (Philippians 2:7). His life revealed perfect obedience to the Father, complete dependence on Scripture, and sacrificial love for others.

To be effective in evangelism, believers must strive to mirror this Christlike character. The message of the gospel calls people to conform to Christ's image, and the messenger must exemplify that transformation. The world is more likely to listen to a Christlike life than to empty rhetoric.

Humility

Humility is the foundation of all godly character. The evangelist must never see himself as superior to those he seeks to reach. He is not the source of salvation but merely its servant. Scripture declares, "God is opposed to the proud, but gives grace to the humble" (James 4:6). Pride alienates both God and man; humility draws both near.

The humble evangelist acknowledges his own dependence upon Jehovah. He gives glory to God for every success and takes responsibility for his failures. Paul, though one of the greatest evangelists in history, called himself "the least of the apostles" and "the chief of sinners" (1 Corinthians 15:9; 1 Timothy 1:15). Such humility did not weaken his ministry; it strengthened it, for it magnified the grace of God.

Humility also manifests in a teachable spirit. The evangelist must remain open to correction and growth. He must listen as well as speak, showing respect for others even when they disagree. A humble messenger is a credible witness to a humble Savior.

Compassion

Compassion moves the evangelist to reach out to those lost in sin. Without compassion, evangelism becomes mechanical and self-serving. Jesus' ministry was marked by deep compassion for the multitudes, "because they were distressed and dispirited like sheep without a shepherd" (Matthew 9:36). His heart broke for those enslaved by false religion and moral darkness.

True compassion sees beyond outward rebellion to inward need. It recognizes that sinners are victims of deception, ensnared by Satan, and in desperate need of deliverance. The compassionate evangelist does not condemn but pleads, not despising the lost but yearning for their salvation.

Compassion also requires patience. The evangelist must understand that conversion is often a process. He must be willing to sow seeds, water them with prayer, and wait for God to give the increase. A harsh or impatient attitude contradicts the very gospel he proclaims.

Love

Love is the supreme virtue of the evangelist. It is the motive, method, and mark of true ministry. Paul declared, "The love of Christ controls us" (2 Corinthians 5:14). Without love, all preaching, knowledge, and zeal are worthless (1 Corinthians 13:1–3).

Love drives the evangelist to seek the salvation of others, not for personal recognition, but out of sincere concern for their eternal destiny. It compels him to endure rejection, ridicule, and hardship for the sake of those who need Christ. Love does not manipulate or coerce; it persuades gently, honors conscience, and respects free will.

This love must reflect Jehovah's love—holy, selfless, and redemptive. It is not sentimental tolerance of sin, but genuine desire for sinners to be reconciled to God. The evangelist who loves as Christ loved will speak truth even when it offends, and show mercy even when it is undeserved.

Courage

Evangelism requires courage because it often invites opposition. The gospel confronts human pride, exposes sin, and challenges false belief. The evangelist must stand firm in truth, even when it brings ridicule or persecution.

Paul exemplified such courage. He faced imprisonment, beatings, and rejection, yet he declared, "I am not ashamed of the gospel" (Romans 1:16). His boldness did not arise from self-confidence but from trust in Jehovah's power.

Courage does not mean the absence of fear but the triumph of faith over fear. The evangelist must remember that Christ promised, "I am with you always, even to the end of the age" (Matthew 28:20). This assurance gives strength to speak when silence seems safer.

True courage also involves moral integrity. The evangelist must stand for truth not only in preaching but in living. It takes courage to reject compromise, to speak against false teaching, and to maintain purity in a corrupt world.

Authenticity

Authenticity is the harmony between message and life. The authentic evangelist is genuine in faith, transparent in conduct, and consistent in obedience. He does not project an image of perfection but demonstrates sincerity, humility, and repentance.

Hypocrisy destroys credibility. Jesus warned against those who "say things and do not do them" (Matthew 23:3). The world quickly recognizes inconsistency and dismisses the message when the messenger lacks integrity. Authenticity, however, draws others to the truth.

The authentic evangelist lives what he preaches. His family, neighbors, and co-workers see evidence of transformation. His integrity is not confined to public ministry but extends to private life. Such authenticity gives weight to his words and displays the reality of the gospel's power.

The Fruit of the Spirit and Evangelism

The fruit of the Spirit, as described in Galatians 5:22–23, forms the moral foundation of effective evangelism. These virtues—love, joy, peace, patience, kindness, goodness, faithfulness, gentleness, and self-control—manifest the work of the Spirit through the Word in the life of the believer.

Love compels the evangelist to reach out; joy sustains him in adversity; peace anchors his confidence in God's sovereignty; patience enables him to wait for results; kindness and goodness make his message attractive; faithfulness ensures consistency; gentleness makes his correction gracious; and self-control guards his integrity.

The evangelist who lacks these fruits may still speak truth, but his message will lack fragrance. The one who possesses them becomes a living witness to the transforming power of the gospel. The fruit of the Spirit turns evangelism from mere proclamation into demonstration—a visible reflection of Christ's presence in the believer's life.

Conclusion

The effectiveness of evangelism depends as much on the messenger's character as on the message proclaimed. Jehovah chooses to work through holy vessels—men and women whose hearts are pure, motives sincere, and lives aligned with His truth. The evangelist must therefore strive daily to cultivate humility, compassion, love, courage, and authenticity, all rooted in a Christlike spirit.

When the message of the gospel is proclaimed by a messenger who lives it, the world sees not just words but living proof that Jesus Christ changes lives. The character of the evangelist is the living echo of the message he preaches—an unspoken sermon that prepares hearts to hear and believe the Word of God.

CHAPTER 6 Understanding Your Audience: The Wisdom of Reaching Hearts Through Truth

Effective evangelism does not begin with eloquence but with understanding. The evangelist who truly seeks to reach others must first learn to understand those to whom he speaks. Evangelism is not the mere transfer of information—it is the spiritual communication of God's truth to human hearts. To accomplish this, the evangelist must discern the condition of his audience, their beliefs, their fears, and the barriers that prevent them from embracing the gospel. Understanding one's audience does not mean altering the message to suit them; it means presenting Jehovah's unchanging truth with clarity, compassion, and wisdom so that it pierces through misunderstanding and reveals the hope of salvation in Jesus Christ.

The Biblical Foundation for Understanding the Audience

Scripture provides numerous examples of God's messengers demonstrating spiritual discernment toward their audiences. Jesus Christ Himself, the perfect evangelist, consistently adapted His approach while maintaining the same message. To the Samaritan woman at the well, He spoke of living water (John 4:10–14). To Nicodemus, He spoke of new birth (John 3:3–7). To the multitudes, He used parables drawn from everyday life—seeds, vineyards, lamps, and nets—to communicate profound spiritual truths. He met people where they were but always led them to where they needed to be.

The apostle Paul also modeled this principle. In Acts 17, when he preached in Athens, he began by acknowledging the Athenians' religiosity, saying, "Men of Athens, I observe that you are very religious in all respects" (Acts 17:22). From there, he exposed their ignorance of the true God and proclaimed the risen Christ. In contrast, when addressing Jews in the synagogue, Paul reasoned from the Scriptures, appealing to their understanding of the Law and the Prophets (Acts 17:2–3).

This adaptability did not compromise truth but expressed wisdom. Paul explained his approach, saying, "I have become all things to all men, so that I may by all means save some" (1 Corinthians 9:22). He never altered the gospel's content but sought to remove unnecessary obstacles so that his hearers could clearly see Christ. The effective evangelist, likewise, studies both Scripture and the soul, learning how to connect the eternal Word to temporal hearts.

Knowing the Spiritual Condition of the Audience

Every person who hears the gospel stands in one of several spiritual conditions—ignorant of truth, indifferent, self-righteous, skeptical, or seeking. Understanding these conditions helps the evangelist to address each appropriately.

The ignorant need teaching. They must hear who Jehovah is, what sin is, and how salvation is offered through Christ. The evangelist must explain patiently and clearly, never assuming prior knowledge.

The indifferent need awakening. They must be confronted with the seriousness of sin and the reality of judgment. The evangelist must speak with urgency and conviction, appealing to conscience rather than curiosity.

The self-righteous need humbling. They must see that their good works cannot save them, for "by the works of the Law no flesh will be justified" (Galatians 2:16). The evangelist must expose pride gently but firmly through the light of Scripture.

The skeptical need reasoned persuasion. They must see the historical and moral credibility of the gospel. Paul reasoned with Felix and Agrippa about righteousness, self-control, and the judgment to come (Acts 24:25; 26:28).

The seeking need guidance. They must be shown the way of salvation clearly, as Philip did for the Ethiopian eunuch, explaining the Scriptures and leading him to faith in Christ (Acts 8:35–38).

Understanding the spiritual condition of the audience allows the evangelist to apply the Word of God accurately—like a physician applying the right medicine for a specific ailment.

Cultural Awareness Without Compromise

The effective evangelist must also understand the cultural environment of his audience. Culture shapes how people think, what they value, and how they interpret truth. Yet while understanding culture is necessary, conforming to it is dangerous. The evangelist must never dilute or distort the gospel to make it more palatable to the culture. Scripture warns, "Do not be conformed to this world, but be transformed by the renewing of your mind" (Romans 12:2).

Cultural understanding enables clarity, not compromise. For instance, in a society that values autonomy, the evangelist can explain that true freedom comes through obedience to Christ (John 8:32–36). In a culture obsessed with material success, he can reveal the emptiness of wealth compared to the eternal riches of salvation (Mark 8:36).

Paul used cultural awareness wisely in Athens by referencing the altar "to an unknown god" as a bridge to proclaim the true God (Acts 17:23). He did not validate their idolatry but redirected their spiritual curiosity toward truth. The modern evangelist must do likewise—use cultural points of contact to guide listeners to Scripture, not away from it.

The Role of Listening in Understanding the Audience

Listening is a spiritual discipline and a vital part of evangelism. The evangelist who listens before speaking reflects the wisdom of Proverbs 18:13: "He who gives an answer before he hears, it is folly and shame to him." Listening demonstrates respect and reveals what obstacles, doubts, or misconceptions prevent a person from understanding the gospel.

Jesus exemplified this when He asked questions to draw out hearts. When the rich young ruler called

Him "Good Teacher," Jesus asked, "Why do you call Me good?" (Mark 10:18), exposing the man's misunderstanding of goodness and deity. Listening enabled Jesus to respond precisely to the individual's spiritual state.

When evangelists listen carefully, they discover the real issues beneath surface objections. A person may raise intellectual challenges, but their true struggle might be moral rebellion or emotional hurt. Understanding these deeper issues allows the evangelist to apply Scripture with precision and compassion.

Communicating Clearly and Graciously

Understanding the audience also involves speaking in a way that is understandable and gracious. Colossians 4:6 instructs believers, "Let your speech always be with grace, as though seasoned with salt, so that you will know how you should respond to each person." The evangelist must communicate the truth of Scripture clearly, avoiding theological jargon or unnecessary complexity.

The message of the gospel is profound but not complicated: that Christ died for our sins, was buried, and rose again. However, the way it is expressed must be adapted to the listener's understanding. To a child, the gospel must be explained simply. To an educated skeptic, it must be presented logically and historically. To the brokenhearted, it must be offered tenderly and personally.

Graceful communication does not mean softening truth; it means delivering truth in love. Harshness alienates, while gentleness invites. The evangelist must speak firmly against sin yet tenderly toward sinners, remembering that the goal is not to win arguments but to win souls.

Recognizing Barriers to Belief

Understanding one's audience also means identifying the barriers that hinder belief. These may be intellectual, emotional, moral, or spiritual. Some reject the gospel because of pride—they do not want to admit their need for forgiveness. Others because of pain—they cannot reconcile their suffering with the goodness of God. Still others because of deception—they have been misled by false religion or worldly philosophy.

The evangelist must address these barriers with patience and Scripture. Intellectual objections require reasoned answers (1 Peter 3:15). Emotional wounds require compassion and prayer. Moral resistance requires a call to repentance. In every case, the solution is not human persuasion but the power of the Word of God to convict and heal.

Adapting Approach Without Altering Truth

Understanding the audience allows the evangelist to adapt his approach while keeping the message pure. The methods may vary, but the gospel remains the same. Jesus used parables, Paul used reasoning, and Peter used direct confrontation. Each approach fit the audience's condition.

The evangelist must be sensitive to timing and tone. Some need gentle instruction; others need bold confrontation. Some need encouragement; others need rebuke. Jude wrote, "Have mercy on some, who are doubting; save others, snatching them out of the fire" (Jude 22–23). Spiritual discernment is essential to know when to comfort and when to confront.

Adapting the approach does not mean adjusting the content. The message of Christ's death, burial, and resurrection is non-negotiable. The art lies in delivering this unchanging truth through channels the listener can understand.

The Role of Empathy in Evangelism

Empathy is the bridge between truth and trust. The evangelist who feels deeply for the lost will speak differently than one who merely performs a duty. Jesus was "moved with compassion" (Matthew 9:36), and that compassion gave authenticity to His words. People listen when they sense genuine concern.

Empathy allows the evangelist to see the sinner not as an enemy but as a soul in need of redemption. It enables him to endure rejection without resentment and to persevere with patience. The gospel is not merely heard through the ears—it is felt through the heart. When love and empathy accompany the message, hearts open more readily to its truth.

The Necessity of Prayer for Understanding

True understanding of the audience does not come merely through observation but through prayer. Only Jehovah can reveal the heart's hidden motives and prepare it to receive truth. The evangelist must pray for discernment—to see beyond words into the soul's real condition.

Paul prayed that God would "open up to us a door for the word" (Colossians 4:3). He understood that only divine intervention can make a heart receptive. Prayer aligns the evangelist with God's will, humbles the heart, and ensures that every word spoken flows from dependence on divine wisdom rather than human judgment.

Prayer also softens the evangelist's heart toward his audience. It removes prejudice, impatience, and pride, replacing them with compassion and humility. Through prayer, the evangelist learns to see people as Jehovah sees them—sheep without a shepherd, desperately in need of grace.

Balancing Truth and Love

Understanding one's audience requires maintaining a perfect balance between truth and love. Truth without love becomes harsh legalism; love without truth becomes sentimental compromise. Jesus embodied both perfectly—He was "full of grace and truth" (John 1:14).

The evangelist must strive for that same balance. He must speak truth uncompromisingly, for the gospel cannot save unless it exposes sin. Yet he must also speak lovingly, for truth without grace cannot heal the wounded soul.

Understanding one's audience means discerning when to confront and when to comfort, when to warn and when to weep. Every encounter must be governed by love for God's glory and love for the lost.

Conclusion

Understanding your audience is essential to effective evangelism. It requires spiritual discernment, patience, compassion, and wisdom guided by Scripture. The evangelist must know not only the message of salvation but also the people who need to hear it. He must listen before he speaks, discern before he declares, and love before he persuades.

Jehovah's truth never changes, but human hearts vary in how they hear it. The wise evangelist studies both—the Word of God and the condition of man—so that he may bridge the distance between divine truth and human need. By understanding his audience, the evangelist becomes a more faithful ambassador of Christ, speaking not just to minds but to hearts, and guiding souls to the One Who alone can save.

CHAPTER 7 All True Christians Are Evangelizers: The Divine Calling of Every Follower of Christ

Evangelism is not a spiritual gift limited to a few; it is the divine responsibility and joyful privilege of every believer. From the beginning of the Christian faith, the command to proclaim the gospel has applied to all who have been redeemed by Christ. Evangelism is not merely the work of pastors, missionaries, or trained speakers—it is the natural outflow of a heart transformed by grace. To know Christ truly is to desire that others know Him as well. Every genuine Christian is called, equipped, and commissioned by Jehovah to bear witness to the salvation that comes through His Son.

The Universal Mandate of Evangelism

The Great Commission was not given to a select class of spiritual leaders but to all disciples of Jesus Christ. In Matthew 28:18–20, Jesus declared, "All authority has been given to Me in heaven and on earth. Go therefore and make disciples of all the nations." This command was addressed to every follower, not just the apostles. The promise that follows—"I am with you always, even to the end of the age"—extends the commission to all believers throughout history.

Similarly, Mark 16:15 records Jesus saying, "Go into all the world and preach the gospel to all creation." The command is absolute and universal. It is not contingent upon age, social status, or spiritual office. Every believer is to be an active participant in the proclamation of the gospel.

Evangelism, therefore, is not an optional expression of faith but an essential mark of true discipleship. A Christian who does not share the message of salvation is living in contradiction to his calling. The gospel was never meant to be hidden but proclaimed. Jesus compared believers to light, saying, "You are the light of the world. A city set on a hill cannot be hidden" (Matthew 5:14). Light exists to illuminate; so must the Christian's life and words reveal the truth of God's salvation.

Evangelism as Evidence of Genuine Faith

All true Christians are evangelizers because genuine faith inevitably expresses itself in witness.

The moment one experiences forgiveness, the natural response is to share it. The Samaritan woman, after encountering Jesus at the well, immediately went to her town and proclaimed, "Come, see a man who told me all the things that I have done; this is not the Christ, is it?" (John 4:29). She was neither trained nor instructed; her testimony flowed from gratitude and conviction.

Likewise, the man delivered from demons in Mark 5 was told by Jesus, "Go home to your people and report to them what great things the Lord has done for you" (Mark 5:19). His first act as a disciple was evangelism. The same holds true for all who have truly encountered Christ. Faith that saves is faith that speaks.

Paul wrote in 2 Corinthians 4:13, "I believed, therefore I spoke." Belief and proclamation are inseparable. The Christian who has experienced redemption cannot remain silent while others perish. The gospel transforms not only the heart but also the mouth—it compels speech.

The Early Church: A Model of Universal Evangelism

The early Church demonstrated that evangelism was the duty and delight of every believer. After the persecution that followed Stephen's death, Acts 8:4 records, "Those who had been scattered went about preaching the word." These were not apostles or clergy—they were ordinary believers forced to flee for their lives, yet everywhere they went, they shared the message of Christ.

This grassroots evangelism transformed the world. The Roman Empire could not silence the spread of the gospel because every believer became a missionary. Their faith was not confined to church gatherings but lived out in homes, marketplaces, and public squares. The Church grew not through official programs but through personal testimony. Every Christian saw himself as a witness.

This pattern must continue today. True Christianity is contagious. When believers genuinely love Christ, they naturally desire to make Him known. Evangelism ceases to be a program and becomes a lifestyle—an expression of gratitude to the Savior and obedience to His command.

The Responsibility of Every Believer

All true Christians bear the responsibility to share the gospel because they have been entrusted with it. Paul described believers as "ambassadors for

Christ" (2 Corinthians 5:20). An ambassador does not choose whether to deliver his message; he speaks on behalf of the One who sent him. The same is true for every Christian. Jehovah has reconciled us to Himself through Christ and now sends us to proclaim that same reconciliation to others.

Jesus said in John 20:21, "As the Father has sent Me, I also send you." Every believer is a representative of Christ in the world. Evangelism is not an optional activity but an essential expression of spiritual obedience. Failure to witness is disobedience to Christ's command and neglect of one's neighbor's eternal need.

James reminds believers that "to one who knows the right thing to do and does not do it, to him it is sin" (James 4:17). Evangelism is not merely good advice; it is the right thing—the most important thing—for those who have been redeemed. To withhold the gospel from others is spiritual negligence.

The Privilege of Evangelism

While evangelism is a responsibility, it is also a profound privilege. Jehovah has chosen to accomplish His redemptive work through human messengers. The Creator of the universe allows believers to participate in His eternal purpose—the salvation of souls. This calling elevates every Christian's daily life. Whether at work, school, or home, each believer stands as a living witness of divine grace.

Paul expressed this awe when he wrote, "We have this treasure in earthen vessels, so that the surpassing greatness of the power will be of God and not from ourselves" (2 Corinthians 4:7). The treasure is the gospel; the earthen vessel is the believer. Evangelism reveals that salvation belongs to Jehovah, yet He graciously allows us to share in the joy of proclaiming it.

There is no greater honor than to speak for Christ. The angels in Heaven rejoice when a sinner repents (Luke 15:10), and believers on earth share in that heavenly joy whenever they lead someone to faith.

The Empowerment for Evangelism

All true Christians are evangelizers because Jehovah has empowered them to be so through His Word. While the Holy Spirit no longer indwells individuals as in the apostolic era, He continues to guide through the inspired Scriptures. The Word of

God equips believers with everything necessary for evangelism—truth, wisdom, and courage.

Paul wrote, "The word of Christ richly dwells within you" (Colossians 3:16). The believer who studies and applies Scripture will be prepared to share it. Evangelism is not about self-confidence but about confidence in the Word of God. Hebrews 4:12 declares that "the word of God is living and active... able to judge the thoughts and intentions of the heart." The evangelist's power lies not in personality but in the truth he proclaims.

Prayer also empowers evangelism. Paul requested, "Pray... that God will open up to us a door for the word" (Colossians 4:3). Every Christian can pray for opportunities, boldness, and the right words to speak. Through prayer and Scripture, Jehovah equips all believers for the work of proclaiming the gospel.

The Motivation for Evangelism

The motivation for evangelism flows from love—love for God and love for others. Jesus said the greatest commandments are to "love the Lord your God with all your heart" and to "love your neighbor as yourself" (Matthew 22:37–39). True love cannot remain silent while others perish in unbelief.

Paul was driven by this love when he wrote, "The love of Christ controls us" (2 Corinthians 5:14). Love for Christ compels the believer to obey His command, and love for others compels him to warn them of judgment and offer them salvation. Evangelism is the highest expression of love—it seeks the eternal good of others above personal comfort or reputation.

The believer who truly loves Jehovah cannot remain silent. As the psalmist declared, "I will not hide Your righteousness within my heart; I will speak of Your faithfulness and Your salvation" (Psalm 40:10). Love gives courage to speak even when it is inconvenient, unpopular, or dangerous.

The Lifestyle of Evangelism

Evangelism is more than occasional witnessing; it is a way of life. Every believer's words, actions, and attitudes should reflect the gospel's truth. Jesus commanded, "Let your light shine before men in such a way that they may see your good works, and glorify your Father who is in heaven" (Matthew 5:16).

A consistent Christian life validates the message of salvation. Hypocrisy discredits the gospel, but integrity makes it attractive. The believer's kindness, honesty, and purity serve as a living sermon to those who observe him. As Peter urged, "Keep your behavior excellent among the Gentiles... so that because of your good deeds... they may glorify God in the day of visitation" (1 Peter 2:12).

However, lifestyle alone is not enough. The gospel must be spoken, for "faith comes from hearing" (Romans 10:17). The believer's conduct prepares the soil, but the Word of God is the seed that produces new life. Every Christian must be both a living example and a verbal witness.

The Reward for Evangelism

Jehovah promises eternal reward for those who faithfully proclaim the gospel. Daniel 12:3 declares, "Those who lead the many to righteousness will shine like the stars forever and ever." The fruit of evangelism is everlasting joy—the privilege of seeing others saved through one's witness.

Paul viewed those he led to Christ as his "joy and crown" (Philippians 4:1). Each soul won to Christ becomes part of the eternal testimony of Jehovah's grace. Even when evangelism seems fruitless, the labor is never in vain. Scripture assures, "Your toil is not in vain in the Lord" (1 Corinthians 15:58).

The Urgency of Evangelism

All true Christians are evangelizers because the task is urgent. Every day, countless souls enter eternity without Christ. The brevity of life and the certainty of judgment demand action. Jesus said, "We must work the works of Him who sent Me as long as it is day; night is coming when no one can work" (John 9:4).

The believer's time on earth is brief, but his opportunity to influence eternity is immeasurable. Evangelism is not something to be delayed until a more convenient time. Now is the acceptable time; today is the day of salvation (2 Corinthians 6:2).

To remain silent while the world perishes is to deny the very purpose of redemption. We were saved not only to worship but to witness—to be living instruments through which others hear the truth.

Conclusion

All true Christians are evangelizers because all true Christians are followers of Christ, and Christ was the ultimate Evangelist. To belong to Him is to share His mission. The redeemed are not spectators but participants in the greatest work ever given—the proclamation of salvation through the death and resurrection of Jesus Christ.

Every believer, regardless of background or ability, has a role in this mission. Some will preach publicly, others will share privately, but all must testify. Evangelism is not a burden but a blessing—a divine privilege to speak of the grace that has saved us. When the Church embraces this truth, it becomes what it was meant to be: a living witness to the nations.

To be a Christian is to be an evangelist. The two cannot be separated. Those who have truly met the Savior will not hide His light—they will shine, speak, and live so that others may come to know the same redemption they have received.

CHAPTER 8 Starting Your Evangelism Journey as a Beginner: Learning to Share the Gospel with Confidence and Faithfulness

Evangelism is the heartbeat of the Christian life. It is the divine command and joyful privilege given to every follower of Jesus Christ—to proclaim the good news of salvation to a lost and dying world. Yet for many believers, especially those just beginning their walk of faith, evangelism can seem daunting. Questions arise: *Where do I start? What do I say? What if I am rejected?* These concerns are natural, but Scripture provides both the instruction and encouragement necessary to begin this journey with confidence and faithfulness. Evangelism is not about human skill or eloquence—it is about obedience to Jehovah's Word, love for others, and trust in the power of the gospel.

Understanding the Purpose of Evangelism

Before beginning the journey of evangelism, every believer must first understand *why* evangelism exists. It is not a church program or optional activity—it is the very mission of every Christian. Jesus Christ commissioned His followers, saying, "Go therefore and make disciples of all the nations" (Matthew 28:19). This command, often called the Great Commission, defines the purpose of the Church and the personal duty of every believer.

Evangelism glorifies Jehovah by revealing His mercy and truth to those who are lost. It is the means through which God extends His invitation to salvation. Paul wrote, "How will they believe in Him whom they have not heard? And how will they hear without a preacher?" (Romans 10:14). Every believer, therefore, is a messenger through whom God reaches others.

The purpose of evangelism is not to argue or to win debates, but to proclaim truth. It is to lovingly present the message that through faith in Christ, sinners can be forgiven, reconciled to God, and receive eternal life. The goal is obedience to God and compassion for the lost, not human approval or recognition.

Overcoming Fear and Inadequacy

The greatest obstacle most beginners face in evangelism is fear—fear of rejection, of failure, or of saying the wrong thing. Yet Scripture assures us that the power of evangelism does not depend on the messenger's ability, but on the message itself. Paul declared, "I am not ashamed of the gospel, for it is the power of God for salvation to everyone who believes" (Romans 1:16).

The gospel itself carries divine power; the evangelist is merely the vessel. Jehovah uses weak and ordinary people to accomplish extraordinary purposes so that all glory belongs to Him. When Moses hesitated to speak before Pharaoh, God reminded him, "Who has made man's mouth? ... Now then go, and I, even I, will be with your mouth" (Exodus 4:11–12). The same promise applies to every believer who speaks for Christ.

Courage in evangelism comes from confidence in God's Word, not in oneself. As a beginner, remember that your responsibility is faithfulness, not results. Salvation is God's work; your duty is to plant and water the seed (1 Corinthians 3:6–7). The rest belongs to Him.

Preparing Your Heart Before You Speak

Effective evangelism begins not with speaking but with spiritual preparation. Before sharing the gospel with others, believers must examine their own hearts before God. The evangelist's message must flow from a life transformed by grace.

David prayed, "Search me, O God, and know my heart... and lead me in the everlasting way" (Psalm 139:23–24). The same prayer must precede every act of witnessing. A heart burdened with sin or pride cannot effectively represent Christ. Purity, humility, and love prepare the believer to speak with sincerity and conviction.

Prayer is essential. Ask Jehovah to give you wisdom, compassion, and boldness. Pray for open doors, receptive hearts, and the right words. Paul requested prayer from the Colossians "that God will open up to us a door for the word" (Colossians 4:3). Evangelism begins on your knees before it ever begins with your mouth.

Knowing the Message You Proclaim

Before sharing the gospel, every evangelist must know it clearly and confidently. The message of salvation is simple yet profound:

1. **God is holy**—He is the Creator and Sovereign of all things, perfectly righteous and just (Isaiah 6:3).

2. **Man is sinful**—All have sinned and fall short of the glory of God (Romans 3:23). Sin separates humanity from Jehovah and results in death (Romans 6:23).

3. **Christ is Savior**—Jesus, God's Son, lived a sinless life, died on the cross for our sins, and rose again to provide redemption and reconciliation (1 Corinthians 15:3–4).

4. **Salvation is by faith**—Forgiveness and eternal life are received through repentance and faith in Jesus Christ alone (Ephesians 2:8–9).

This is the gospel—the "good news." Every believer must be able to express it in their own words with clarity and conviction. A beginner does not need advanced theological training; he simply needs to understand and communicate what Christ has done for him personally. Your testimony—how God saved and changed you—is one of your most powerful tools in evangelism.

Starting with Those Around You

The journey of evangelism begins right where you are. You do not need to travel across the world to obey Christ's command. Your family, friends, neighbors, and co-workers form your first mission field. Jesus told the healed man in Mark 5:19, "Go home to your people and report to them what great things the Lord has done for you."

Begin by sharing the gospel naturally in everyday conversations. Look for opportunities to speak of spiritual things—when someone mentions fear, injustice, or purpose, point them to Christ. Avoid forcing the conversation; instead, let it flow from genuine interest and love.

You may also give out gospel tracts, share Scripture verses, or invite others to read the Bible with you. Each small act of witness plants a seed that God can cause to grow. Do not underestimate the power of consistent, simple testimony.

Learning to Listen

A wise evangelist listens more than he speaks. Listening reveals the heart's condition and shows respect for the other person. It demonstrates that you care not only about their conversion but about their soul. Proverbs 18:13 warns, "He who gives an answer before he hears, it is folly and shame to him."

When you listen, you learn what obstacles prevent belief—whether ignorance, pride, pain, or confusion. Respond with Scripture, not opinion. Jesus often asked questions that revealed truth: "What do you seek?" "Who do you say that I am?" "Do you believe this?" His example teaches us to guide others gently toward reflection and repentance.

Relying on Scripture

Scripture is the foundation of all evangelism. It is the Word of God that convicts hearts, not human reasoning. Hebrews 4:12 declares that "the word of God is living and active and sharper than any two-edged sword." As a beginner, make it your goal to memorize key verses that explain the gospel clearly, such as:

- **John 3:16:** "For God so loved the world, that He gave His only begotten Son, that whoever believes in Him shall not perish, but have eternal life."

- **Romans 3:23:** "All have sinned and fall short of the glory of God."
- **Romans 6:23:** "The wages of sin is death, but the free gift of God is eternal life in Christ Jesus our Lord."
- **Romans 10:9:** "If you confess with your mouth Jesus as Lord, and believe in your heart that God raised Him from the dead, you will be saved."

When you use Scripture, you speak with divine authority. The Word carries its own power, even when the listener does not immediately respond. Your task is to present it faithfully; God will do the rest.

Dealing with Rejection

Every beginner in evangelism must expect and accept rejection. Jesus Himself was despised and rejected by men (Isaiah 53:3). He warned His disciples, "If they persecuted Me, they will also persecute you" (John 15:20). The rejection of the message is not a rejection of you personally but of Christ.

Do not be discouraged when others ignore, mock, or oppose your witness. Remember, even the greatest evangelists faced hostility. Your duty is to remain faithful. Paul reminded Timothy to "preach the word... with great patience and instruction" (2 Timothy 4:2). Continue to pray for those who reject the message, and trust that Jehovah may yet soften their hearts in time.

Cultivating a Heart for the Lost

Successful evangelism begins with compassion. Before speaking to men about God, speak to God about men. Pray for the lost with genuine concern, remembering that apart from Christ they face eternal destruction. Jesus wept over Jerusalem, saying, "How often I wanted to gather your children together... and you were unwilling" (Matthew 23:37). Such compassion must fill the heart of every believer.

Ask Jehovah to give you His love for sinners. When love motivates you, fear disappears. The desire to see others saved outweighs the discomfort of speaking up. Evangelism becomes not a duty but a delight—a natural outflow of love for God and neighbor.

Growing Through Experience

Evangelism, like any spiritual discipline, grows through practice. The more you share your faith, the more natural and confident you become. Do not wait until you feel "ready"; begin now, trusting God to guide you. Every conversation teaches you something—how to listen better, how to explain more clearly, how to respond with grace.

Learn from both successes and mistakes. Reflect on what worked, what didn't, and how you can improve. Stay humble and open to growth. Evangelism is not a performance but a journey of learning and faith.

Finding Encouragement in the Church

No believer is called to evangelize alone. The local church exists as a body of encouragement and partnership. Seek fellowship with other believers who share your passion for witnessing. Pray together, share experiences, and support one another. The book of Acts portrays believers united in mission—praying, preaching, and rejoicing together in the spread of the gospel.

Church leaders also play a vital role in equipping believers for evangelism. Ephesians 4:12 states that pastors and teachers are given "for the equipping of the holy ones for the work of service." Attend evangelism training, participate in outreach, and learn from those more experienced in sharing the faith.

Trusting Jehovah with the Results

The beginner in evangelism must always remember that success is not measured by visible results but by faithfulness to God's call. You may never see the fruit of your efforts in this life, but the Word of God never returns empty (Isaiah 55:11). Some will plant, others will water, and God will give the growth.

Evangelism is not about numbers—it is about obedience. The ultimate goal is to glorify Jehovah by proclaiming His truth, whether one person believes or many. The joy of evangelism is found in obedience itself, knowing that you have been faithful to your Lord's command.

Conclusion

Starting your evangelism journey as a beginner is both a challenge and a privilege. You may feel unprepared, but Jehovah equips those who obey. You may fear rejection, but Christ is with you always. You may speak to only one person, but Heaven rejoices over even one sinner who repents (Luke 15:10).

Begin where you are. Speak the truth with love. Trust God's Word, rely on prayer, and cultivate compassion for the lost. Evangelism is not about perfection—it is about faithfulness. As you step forward in obedience, you will discover the joy of being used by Jehovah to bring eternal hope to others.

CHAPTER 9 Street-Level Witness: Sharing Faith in Everyday Encounters

Evangelism is not confined to pulpits, mission fields, or formal programs. It takes place wherever Christians live, work, and interact with others. Street-level witness is the expression of the gospel in ordinary moments—at the marketplace, in a conversation with a neighbor, at the workplace, or while walking down a city street. This kind of evangelism reflects the reality that every believer is a missionary wherever Jehovah has placed him. The streets, parks, cafés, and sidewalks of our communities are not random settings; they are the very mission fields in which the light of Christ must shine.

Street-level evangelism is the heartbeat of biblical witness—it is spontaneous, personal, and rooted in love. It transforms daily encounters into divine appointments. When Christians recognize that every moment may be an opportunity to proclaim the gospel, their lives become continuous testimonies of grace.

The Biblical Foundation of Everyday Evangelism

Jesus Christ Himself practiced what could be called "street-level evangelism." He met people where they were—in fields, homes, villages, and marketplaces. He spoke to fishermen on the shore, tax collectors at their tables, and beggars along the road. He engaged individuals in ordinary situations and revealed eternal truth through familiar experiences.

In John 4, Jesus met the Samaritan woman at a well, turning a simple request for water into a profound discussion about salvation. In Luke 19, He called Zacchaeus down from a tree and transformed his life over a meal. In Matthew 9, He invited a tax collector to follow Him. Jesus' ministry was not confined to the synagogue; it was woven into the fabric of daily life.

The apostles followed the same pattern. In Acts 17, Paul reasoned with philosophers in the marketplace. In Acts 8, Philip met an Ethiopian official on the road. Street-level evangelism was the normal expression of faith in the early Church. Wherever believers went, they shared Christ. Acts 8:4 records, "Those who had been scattered went about preaching the word."

This same calling remains for every Christian today. The message is unchanged, and the mission continues—not only from pulpits, but from one heart to another in the flow of ordinary life.

The Mission Field Around You

Every Christian lives amid a mission field. The people we encounter daily—neighbors, co-workers, store clerks, delivery drivers, classmates, and strangers—represent souls who may never enter a church building or hear a sermon. Street-level evangelism bridges that gap.

Jesus said to His disciples, "Lift up your eyes and look on the fields, that they are white for harvest" (John 4:35). The harvest field is not distant; it surrounds us. Every city street, rural path, and suburban neighborhood contains people longing for hope. Many are weary, confused, and spiritually lost, yet they cross our paths by divine appointment.

Recognizing this truth transforms the believer's perspective. Every interaction becomes purposeful. The believer who sees life through the lens of evangelism will never encounter a "random" moment. Each day becomes an opportunity to reveal the grace of God through word and deed.

Living as a Witness Before Speaking as a Witness

Street-level evangelism begins with how you live before it extends to what you say. Jesus declared, "You are the light of the world" (Matthew 5:14). Light does not argue with darkness; it simply shines. The consistent character of a Christian—kindness, honesty, purity, and humility—prepares the soil of the heart for the seed of the gospel.

People often observe how believers handle pressure, disappointment, or success long before they listen to what they say. A gentle response, an act of patience, or a word of encouragement can open the door to a gospel conversation. As Peter instructed, "Keep your behavior excellent among the Gentiles... so that they may because of your good deeds glorify God" (1 Peter 2:12).

Street-level witness therefore begins with daily integrity. A believer who lives differently from the world will naturally draw curiosity. Once the life of Christ is seen, the message of Christ can be heard.

Turning Everyday Conversations into Gospel Encounters

The essence of street-level evangelism lies in turning ordinary conversations into opportunities for spiritual discussion. Jesus did this masterfully. He began with what was familiar—water, bread, farming, or fishing—and led His listeners to eternal truth.

Believers today can follow this same pattern. When someone expresses worry, speak of the peace Christ gives. When a friend mentions injustice, explain that only God's righteousness can set the world right. When someone talks about death, speak of resurrection hope. Everyday topics often provide natural bridges to the gospel.

The evangelist does not need to force a conversation. The goal is not to dominate but to direct—to move naturally from the temporal to the eternal. The Holy Spirit uses these moments to awaken hearts. The believer's task is to be ready and willing. As 1 Peter 3:15 exhorts, "Always be ready to make a defense to everyone who asks you to give an account for the hope that is in you, yet with gentleness and reverence."

Compassion as the Heart of Street-Level Evangelism

At the heart of all evangelism lies compassion. Jesus' ministry was driven by compassion for the lost. Matthew 9:36 says, "He felt compassion for them, because they were distressed and dispirited like sheep without a shepherd." Street-level evangelism flows from the same heart—a love that sees beyond sin to the soul in need of grace.

Compassion removes barriers. It enables the believer to see people not as opponents but as potential brothers and sisters in Christ. It transforms inconvenience into opportunity and discomfort into joy. Compassionate evangelism is patient and kind. It listens before it speaks, prays before it argues, and loves before it corrects.

A cold, mechanical approach to evangelism may communicate facts, but it will not win hearts. The world must not only hear that God loves them; they must see that His people do. Genuine concern for others' eternal destiny gives credibility to every word spoken.

The Simplicity of the Gospel Message

Street-level evangelism thrives on simplicity. The gospel is profound, yet it must be expressed plainly so that anyone can understand. A street corner, café, or workplace conversation is not the setting for theological complexity but for clear proclamation.

The message is timeless: humanity is sinful and separated from God (Romans 3:23); sin leads to death (Romans 6:23); Christ died for sinners and rose again (1 Corinthians 15:3–4); and those who repent and believe in Him receive forgiveness and eternal life (John 3:16).

Every believer should know how to express this message concisely, with Scripture as the foundation. Personal testimony enhances it—explaining how Christ's truth has changed your life. The combination of Scripture and sincere experience often touches hearts where argument cannot.

Practical Principles for Street-Level Witness

While every encounter will differ, several principles help guide street-level evangelism:

1. **Be prayerful.** Begin each day asking Jehovah for opportunities to share your faith. Pray for divine appointments and for courage to speak when the moment comes.

2. **Be observant.** Notice people's needs, expressions, and conversations. The Holy Spirit often prompts awareness of who is ready to listen.

3. **Be respectful.** Treat every person with dignity. Even those who mock or reject the gospel are souls created in God's image.

4. **Be gentle but firm.** Speak truth without compromise, yet do so with grace and humility. Avoid arguments; your goal is persuasion, not pride.

5. **Be scriptural.** Let your message flow from the Word of God, not personal philosophy. The authority lies in Scripture, not opinion.

6. **Be patient.** Some seeds take years to grow. You may never see immediate results, but the Word will accomplish its purpose in God's timing.

Facing Opposition and Rejection

Street-level evangelism often invites resistance. The world resists truth because it exposes sin. Jesus warned His followers, "If the world hates you, you know that it has hated Me before it hated you" (John 15:18). Yet opposition must never silence the believer.

Rejection is not a reflection of failure; it is evidence of faithfulness. The prophets were rejected, the apostles persecuted, and Christ Himself crucified. Still, they persevered. The believer must remember that Jehovah measures success not by the number of converts but by the faithfulness of His servants.

Respond to hostility with grace. When cursed, bless. When mocked, pray. When ignored, persevere. The evangelist's strength comes from knowing that God's Word never returns void (Isaiah 55:11).

The Role of Scripture in Street-Level Evangelism

In every encounter, the authority of evangelism is the Word of God. Human reasoning may persuade for a moment, but Scripture penetrates to the heart. Hebrews 4:12 declares that "the word of God is living and active... able to judge the thoughts and intentions of the heart."

Carry the Word with you—not merely in print but in memory. A few well-chosen verses can change an entire conversation. When Jesus confronted temptation in the wilderness, He responded each time with "It is written." Likewise, the believer on the street must rely on Scripture to correct error, reveal truth, and offer hope.

The goal is to let God speak for Himself. Your voice becomes His instrument when you quote His Word.

Building Bridges Through Acts of Kindness

Street-level witness extends beyond words. Simple acts of kindness often open doors that words alone cannot. Offering help to a stranger, showing patience in frustration, or extending forgiveness in conflict demonstrates Christ's love in tangible ways.

Jesus said, "Let your light shine before men... that they may see your good works, and glorify your Father who is in heaven" (Matthew 5:16). Acts of service do not replace the gospel, but they prepare the ground for it. People often need to *see* love before they are ready to *hear* truth.

A smile, a helping hand, or a listening ear can be the spark that ignites a gospel conversation. The believer who lives out compassion earns the right to speak about salvation.

Developing a Lifestyle of Street-Level Evangelism

Street-level witness is not an event but a lifestyle. It means living each day with an awareness of eternity. Evangelism becomes part of who you are, not something you occasionally do.

Begin by dedicating your everyday environment to God's mission. The place where you shop, the route you walk, the café you visit—these become holy ground when approached with evangelistic purpose. Ask Jehovah daily, "Whom will You have me speak to today?"

Evangelism also grows through consistency. When people see you regularly, they begin to notice your faith. Small conversations can lead to deeper discussions over time. The street evangelist sows patiently, trusting that each encounter contributes to God's greater plan.

The Joy and Reward of Street-Level Evangelism

There is no greater joy than leading someone to faith in Christ. Luke 15:7 declares, "There will be more joy in heaven over one sinner who repents than over ninety-nine righteous persons who need no repentance." Street-level evangelism allows believers to participate in that heavenly celebration.

Even when conversions are not visible, the evangelist rejoices in obedience. Isaiah's calling was to preach to a hardened people, yet he obeyed faithfully. Likewise, every act of witness glorifies Jehovah, whether the result is conversion or rejection.

Street-level evangelism brings deep spiritual growth. It strengthens faith, increases love for others, and deepens dependence upon God. As you speak of His grace to others, you are reminded daily of the grace that saved you.

Conclusion

Street-level witness transforms ordinary life into sacred opportunity. It turns sidewalks into pulpits, conversations into ministries, and daily routines into acts of eternal significance. Every believer is called to live as an evangelist—ready to share Christ's truth in the flow of ordinary life.

To share faith in everyday encounters is to follow the example of Christ Himself, Who came to seek and to save the lost wherever He found them. The city streets, suburban sidewalks, and quiet country paths all echo the same need—the need for the gospel of salvation.

When believers see every encounter as a divine appointment, they become living messengers of hope in a world of darkness. Street-level evangelism is not about standing on corners with slogans; it is about standing in grace and truth wherever you are, pointing others to the Savior Who alone can give them life.

Edward D. Andrews

CHAPTER 10 Digital Disciples: Evangelism in the Age of Social Media

The twenty-first century has brought unprecedented opportunities for communication. The world is now connected in ways unimaginable to earlier generations. Social media platforms—once mere tools for personal expression and entertainment—have become the global public square. Every day, billions of people gather online to share opinions, stories, and experiences. For the Christian, this reality presents both a challenge and an opportunity. Evangelism, once confined to physical spaces, now extends into the vast digital realm. The same message that Jesus commanded His followers to proclaim to "all nations" (Matthew 28:19) can now travel instantly across borders and languages through the power of technology. Thus, in this generation, every believer is called to become a *digital disciple*—a faithful witness for Christ in the online world.

The Expanding Mission Field of the Digital Age

Social media represents the largest mission field in human history. Platforms such as Facebook, Instagram, X (formerly Twitter), YouTube, and others host billions of souls searching for identity, purpose, and truth. Many spend more hours engaging online than interacting face-to-face. In this environment of constant communication, the command of Christ to proclaim the gospel "to the remotest part of the earth" (Acts 1:8) takes on new immediacy.

The digital world mirrors the ancient marketplaces where Paul reasoned daily with those who happened to be present (Acts 17:17). Today's digital forums—comment threads, group chats, and video platforms—function in similar ways. They are arenas of ideas where people exchange beliefs, express doubts, and seek meaning. Just as Paul entered the cultural and intellectual centers of his time, Christians today must enter the online spaces where people gather, bringing the unchanging message of the gospel.

However, this digital mission field demands discernment. The anonymity and accessibility of the internet allow both truth and error to spread rapidly.

The believer must therefore use this platform wisely, not to blend with the noise of the world, but to shine the light of Christ with clarity and grace.

The Biblical Mandate for Digital Evangelism

Though the Bible does not mention modern technology, its principles clearly apply. Jesus commanded His followers to let their light shine before others (Matthew 5:16). That command transcends time and medium. Wherever there are people—whether in ancient streets or digital networks—the Christian must be a witness.

Paul used every means available to communicate the gospel. He traveled across continents, wrote letters, and adapted his message to various audiences without compromising its truth. Were he living today, he would undoubtedly see social media as another means of fulfilling his mission. His statement in 1 Corinthians 9:22–23 summarizes the heart of digital evangelism: "I have become all things to all men, so that I may by all means save some. I do all things for the sake of the gospel."

Digital discipleship is not about technology; it is about faithfulness. The medium changes, but the message remains the same—salvation through the death and resurrection of Jesus Christ.

The Opportunity and Responsibility of Every Believer

Social media grants every believer a voice that can reach far beyond geographical limits. In earlier generations, only preachers, missionaries, or writers could reach the masses. Today, every Christian with a phone or computer can become a global witness. This privilege brings responsibility.

Each post, comment, or message carries influence. Words typed on a screen can build or destroy, bless or curse, edify or offend. Scripture warns, "Death and life are in the power of the tongue" (Proverbs 18:21)—and in our age, that power extends through every keystroke. Digital disciples must therefore speak as representatives of Christ.

Colossians 4:6 commands, "Let your speech always be with grace, as though seasoned with salt." Grace must govern every online interaction. The goal of digital evangelism is not to win arguments but to win souls. Every believer who uses social media bears the name of Christ publicly. Therefore, his words and conduct must reflect His character.

The Message Remains Unchanged

The gospel cannot be modernized. Technology changes rapidly, but the truth of Scripture stands forever. Isaiah 40:8 declares, "The grass withers, the flower fades, but the word of our God stands forever." Digital evangelism must therefore resist the temptation to adapt the gospel to the trends or values of the online world.

Some seek to attract attention by reshaping the message to suit popular culture—offering entertainment, shallow inspiration, or self-help disguised as Christianity. But such distortions betray the gospel's authority. The true message remains: all have sinned (Romans 3:23); sin brings death (Romans 6:23); Jesus Christ died for our sins and rose again (1 Corinthians 15:3–4); and salvation comes only through repentance and faith in Him.

The task of the digital disciple is not to make the message trendy but to make it known. The timeless truth of the gospel must be communicated with clarity and conviction amid the ever-changing currents of the internet.

Using Digital Platforms for the Glory of God

Every social media platform offers unique opportunities for evangelism. A short video may proclaim a biblical truth; a thoughtful post may explain a verse of Scripture; a private message may lead to a life-changing conversation. The goal is not self-promotion but Christ-exaltation.

1 Corinthians 10:31 reminds believers, "Whether, then, you eat or drink or whatever you do, do all to the glory of God." The believer's online presence must therefore glorify God. Profile pages, photos, comments, and shared content should all reflect Christ's character. A digital disciple does not use social media to gain followers for himself but to point others to the Savior.

Digital evangelism can take many forms: posting Bible verses with explanations, sharing testimonies of salvation, responding graciously to questions about faith, creating content that defends biblical truth, or simply expressing Christlike kindness in conversations. Each act becomes a digital seed that God may cause to grow in hearts around the world.

The Character of the Digital Disciple

Before a believer can represent Christ effectively online, his heart must be right before God. The principles of personal holiness and humility that apply to face-to-face evangelism apply equally in the digital realm. The evangelist's character gives credibility to his message.

James 1:19–20 offers essential wisdom for digital communication: "Everyone must be quick to hear, slow to speak and slow to anger; for the anger of man does not achieve the righteousness of God." Online discussions often ignite hostility, pride, and division. The digital disciple must resist these impulses. Truth must always be spoken in love (Ephesians 4:15).

Authenticity is also crucial. People are drawn not to perfection but to sincerity. Sharing one's struggles, testimonies, and lessons learned through Scripture can communicate the reality of faith in a relatable way. However, authenticity must never cross into vanity or self-focus. Every post should exalt Christ, not self.

Balancing Boldness and Grace in Online Evangelism

The digital world rewards controversy, but the gospel requires grace. While boldness is necessary to confront error and proclaim truth, it must always be balanced with gentleness. Paul urged Timothy to correct those in opposition "with gentleness, if perhaps God may grant them repentance" (2 Timothy 2:25).

Digital disciples must therefore learn to communicate with conviction and compassion. Arguments rarely convert hearts; truth spoken with humility often does. When encountering opposition, mockery, or skepticism, respond as Christ did—with steadfastness, patience, and love. The goal is not to prove others wrong but to point them to the One who can make them right with God.

Avoiding the Pitfalls of the Digital Mission Field

The online world is both powerful and perilous. The same platforms that allow evangelism can also tempt believers into pride, distraction, and compromise. Digital disciples must guard their motives and discipline their time.

Social media can easily become a stage for self-promotion rather than gospel proclamation. Jesus warned, "Beware of practicing your righteousness before men to be noticed by them" (Matthew 6:1). The motive for online witness must always be love for God and others—not the pursuit of likes, followers, or recognition.

Furthermore, believers must exercise discernment in what they share. False teachings and worldly ideologies spread rapidly online. Digital disciples must know Scripture well enough to distinguish truth from error. They must also be careful not to engage in fruitless debates that generate more heat than light. Paul warned Titus to "avoid foolish controversies... for they are unprofitable and worthless" (Titus 3:9).

The Power of Testimony in Digital Evangelism

One of the most effective tools in digital evangelism is personal testimony. When believers share how Jehovah's grace has changed their lives, others take notice. The apostle John wrote, "They overcame him because of the blood of the Lamb and because of the word of their testimony" (Revelation 12:11).

A short video or written post describing how Christ delivered you from sin or gave you peace in suffering can reach thousands. Authentic stories cut through cynicism. People may debate doctrine, but they cannot deny a transformed life. Your testimony becomes a living proclamation of the gospel's power.

Building Online Relationships for Eternal Impact

Digital evangelism is most effective when it builds real relationships. Jesus did not preach to crowds alone; He engaged individuals. Likewise, believers can use social media to form genuine spiritual connections—answering questions, offering prayer, and guiding others to Scripture.

Private messages, online Bible studies, and virtual discipleship groups can all nurture faith. The goal is not merely to post truth publicly but to walk alongside seekers personally. The digital disciple acts as a bridge between online witness and real-world transformation.

Prayer: The Engine of Digital Evangelism

As with all forms of evangelism, prayer is the foundation of success. The digital disciple must depend upon Jehovah's power to open hearts. Technology can transmit words, but only God's Spirit can transform souls.

Before posting, pray. Before responding, pray. Before engaging in a conversation, pray for wisdom and grace. Paul's request remains timeless: "Pray… that God will open up to us a door for the word" (Colossians 4:3). Each online encounter is a potential door for the gospel. Prayer ensures that the evangelist enters those doors with divine guidance.

The Eternal Perspective of Digital Evangelism

Digital evangelism is not about temporary impact but eternal consequence. Every post, message, or video may influence a soul's destiny. The believer must remember that behind every screen is a person—a soul created in God's image, in need of salvation.

When Jesus said, "The fields are white for harvest" (John 4:35), those fields now include digital ones. The gospel sown online can reach people who would never meet a missionary in person. Countless testimonies already confirm this truth—people in closed nations hearing the gospel through online videos, individuals in despair finding hope through a social media post, and seekers discovering Christ through digital conversations.

The internet, though often filled with darkness, can also carry the light of Christ. The responsibility rests with His people to use it wisely and faithfully.

Conclusion

In the age of social media, evangelism has entered a new frontier. Every believer has the opportunity to speak truth to the nations from the palm of his hand. Digital discipleship is not about technology—it is about obedience to the timeless command of Christ to "go and make disciples."

To be a digital disciple is to use every tool available for the glory of God, to speak with grace and truth in an online world of confusion, and to shine the light of the gospel where it is most needed. When Christians harness technology for the purposes of Jehovah, the digital world becomes a field of harvest—a place where eternal destinies can change with a single message of hope.

The call is clear: use your voice, your platform, your influence—not for self, but for Christ. In this digital age, the gospel's reach can extend to every corner of the earth. All it requires is willing hearts, faithful witnesses, and the unchanging power of God's Word.

CHAPTER 11 Overcoming Fear: Bold Steps to Proclaim the Good News

Fear has silenced more voices than persecution ever could. Many Christians deeply desire to share the gospel, yet they hesitate, held captive by fear—fear of rejection, ridicule, inadequacy, or confrontation. This fear, though powerful, is not from God. Scripture declares plainly, "For God has not given us a spirit of timidity, but of power and love and sound judgment" (2 Timothy 1:7). Evangelism requires courage, not self-confidence, but confidence in the truth and power of Jehovah's Word. To proclaim the good news is to participate in the very mission of Christ, Who said, "As the Father has sent Me, I also send you" (John 20:21). The path to overcoming fear begins not with emotion, but with conviction—believing that the gospel is worth proclaiming at any cost.

The Nature of Fear in Evangelism

Fear is a natural human reaction to the unknown. When believers contemplate sharing their faith, they often imagine negative outcomes: rejection by friends, awkward conversations, or being labeled as judgmental. Satan uses this fear to suppress the witness of God's people, whispering lies that the gospel will offend or that the believer is unqualified to speak.

Yet Scripture teaches that the fear of man is a snare (Proverbs 29:25). The fear that keeps believers silent is not humility but bondage. It places human opinion above divine command. The moment we allow fear to dictate obedience, we deny the power of the gospel. True evangelistic courage arises when reverence for God surpasses fear of man. As Peter and John boldly declared before hostile authorities, "We cannot stop speaking about what we have seen and heard" (Acts 4:20).

The Source of Boldness: Faith in Jehovah's Word

Boldness in evangelism does not come from natural personality or confidence in speaking; it comes from faith in the authority of God's Word. When Paul faced fierce opposition, he wrote, "Since we have such a hope, we use great boldness in our speech" (2 Corinthians 3:12). His courage was rooted not in himself but in the certainty of the message.

The believer's boldness grows when he understands the divine origin and power of Scripture. The Word of God is not merely persuasive—it is living, active, and able to convict the heart (Hebrews 4:12). The gospel carries within it the power to save (Romans 1:16). When the evangelist realizes that it is Jehovah Himself Who speaks through His Word, fear loses its hold. The messenger's task is to deliver truth; the Spirit's task is to transform hearts through that truth.

Every Christian can proclaim the gospel with confidence because the message, not the messenger, carries the power. Jehovah's Word never returns empty (Isaiah 55:11). Therefore, fear is misplaced; our confidence should rest in God's promise that His truth will accomplish His purpose.

Remembering Who Sends You

When Jesus commissioned His disciples to proclaim the good news, He prefaced the command with an assurance: "All authority has been given to Me in heaven and on earth" (Matthew 28:18). Evangelism is not self-appointed work; it is divine assignment. The one who sends us holds all authority over Heaven, Earth, and every human heart.

This reality removes fear. We are not speaking for ourselves but as ambassadors of the King of Kings (2 Corinthians 5:20). Our duty is representation, not persuasion. Success in evangelism is not measured by conversion but by faithfulness to the One Who sends us.

When Moses hesitated at his calling, Jehovah assured him, "I will be with your mouth and teach you what you are to say" (Exodus 4:12). The same promise holds for every believer today. God equips those He sends. The evangelist's courage flows from the awareness that he is never alone. Christ's final words still echo: "I am with you always, even to the end of the age" (Matthew 28:20).

Confronting the Lies That Feed Fear

To overcome fear, believers must confront the lies that sustain it. Satan's primary strategy is deception—convincing Christians that their witness is futile, their knowledge insufficient, or their words unwelcome. Each of these lies must be countered with biblical truth.

Lie #1: "I don't know enough." Evangelism is not an academic debate; it is the proclamation of truth. The Samaritan woman at the well did not attend theological training, yet she told her village, "Come, see a man who told me all the things that I have done" (John 4:29). Knowledge is important, but the gospel's power lies not in eloquence but in truth. If you know that Christ has saved you, you know enough to tell others.

Lie #2: "People will reject me." Jesus promised rejection. "If the world hates you, you know that it has hated Me before it hated you" (John 15:18). Rejection is not failure; it is confirmation that you stand with Christ. The responsibility to respond belongs to the listener, not the messenger.

Lie #3: "It's not the right time." Procrastination is one of Satan's most effective tools. Yet Scripture commands, "Preach the word; be ready in season and out of season" (2 Timothy 4:2). There is no wrong time to obey God's command. The right time to speak truth is always now.

When believers replace lies with truth, fear begins to lose its power.

The Role of Prayer in Overcoming Fear

Prayer is the believer's greatest weapon against fear. It shifts focus from self to God. When the early Church faced threats, they did not pray for safety but for boldness. Acts 4:29 records their prayer: "And now, Lord, take note of their threats, and grant that Your bond-servants may speak Your word with all confidence." The result was immediate: "They were all filled with the Holy Spirit and began to speak the word of God with boldness" (Acts 4:31).

Prayer aligns the heart with God's purpose. It reminds the evangelist that courage is not an emotion but a gift granted through faith. Each time fear arises, turn it into prayer: "Jehovah, give me strength to speak Your truth." Through such dependence, fear is replaced by peace, and hesitation by resolve.

The Example of Biblical Courage

The pages of Scripture overflow with examples of those who overcame fear to proclaim truth.

Moses feared speaking before Pharaoh, yet by faith he led a nation out of bondage. **Jeremiah** trembled before hostile crowds, yet he declared God's Word faithfully, saying, "His word is in my heart like a burning fire shut up in my bones" (Jeremiah 20:9). **Peter and John**, once fearful and silent during Jesus' arrest, became bold preachers after the resurrection, willing to face imprisonment for their witness.

Paul, beaten and persecuted, declared, "Woe is me if I do not preach the gospel!" (1 Corinthians 9:16).

Their courage did not come from temperament but from trust in Jehovah. The same God Who empowered them empowers believers today. His presence transforms fear into faithfulness.

Love as the Antidote to Fear

The key to overcoming fear is not greater willpower but greater love. 1 John 4:18 declares, "There is no fear in love; but perfect love casts out fear." When love for God and for the lost outweighs fear of rejection, boldness naturally follows.

Jesus' compassion for sinners drove Him to the cross. Paul's love for his people made him willing to be "accursed" for their sake (Romans 9:3). Likewise, the evangelist who truly loves others cannot remain silent. Love sees beyond discomfort to eternal reality. To withhold the gospel from fear is not humility—it is neglect.

Ask Jehovah to deepen your love for the lost. When the heart burns with compassion, courage becomes inevitable. The believer no longer sees evangelism as a duty but as an act of mercy—offering life to those perishing without Christ.

Practical Steps to Build Courage

1. **Meditate on God's promises.** Read passages that affirm His presence and power (Isaiah 41:10, Joshua 1:9, Matthew 28:20). Fear fades when faith is fed.

2. **Start small.** Share your testimony with a friend, co-worker, or family member. Boldness grows through obedience in small steps.

3. **Memorize key Scriptures.** Knowing the Word equips you to speak with confidence. Let Scripture shape your speech and strengthen your resolve.

4. **Partner with others.** Jesus sent His disciples out two by two. Fellowship provides accountability, encouragement, and shared courage.

5. **Focus on obedience, not outcome.** Your responsibility is to speak; God's responsibility is to save. Faithfulness is success in His eyes.

The Power of the Holy Spirit Through the Word

While the indwelling presence of the Spirit is not active today as it was in the apostolic era, the Holy

Spirit continues to empower believers through the inspired Word. Every time a believer opens Scripture, speaks truth, and proclaims Christ, the Spirit's power is at work through the living Word.

This understanding frees the evangelist from self-reliance. The Spirit-inspired Scriptures carry divine energy to convict, convert, and comfort. The believer's boldness, therefore, rests in the certainty that God's Word will never fail. The same Spirit Who inspired the apostles' words operates through those words today when they are faithfully proclaimed.

The Joy of Courageous Evangelism

Courageous evangelism brings deep joy. It draws the believer closer to Jehovah, strengthens faith, and produces eternal fruit. Jesus declared, "Whoever confesses Me before men, I will also confess him before My Father who is in heaven" (Matthew 10:32). To boldly proclaim the gospel is to align oneself publicly with Christ.

Moreover, bold evangelism glorifies God by demonstrating trust in His sovereignty. Every time fear is conquered, the believer testifies that Jehovah is greater than human opposition. The joy of seeing even one sinner repent outweighs every moment of hesitation. Heaven rejoices over each soul saved (Luke 15:7), and the faithful evangelist shares in that joy.

Courage Tested and Rewarded

Courage in evangelism will always be tested. Some will mock; others will listen and reject. But some will believe—and that single soul is worth every moment of fear overcome. Paul, reflecting on his ministry, could say, "I did not shrink from declaring to you the whole purpose of God" (Acts 20:27). May every believer echo those words with a clear conscience.

In eternity, no one will regret having spoken too boldly for Christ. Many, however, will regret having remained silent when opportunities were given. The time to speak is now. The harvest is plentiful, but the laborers are few (Matthew 9:37).

Conclusion

Fear is natural, but faith is supernatural. The believer who trusts in Jehovah's Word, depends on prayer, and acts in love will find courage greater than fear. Bold evangelism is not reckless confidence but reverent obedience. It is the willingness to speak truth because Christ is worthy and because souls are precious.

Overcoming fear in evangelism means seeing the gospel as more powerful than rejection, the mission as more urgent than comfort, and the Lord as more deserving than self. Jehovah has not called His people to silence but to proclamation—to shine light in darkness and to declare salvation through His Son.

When you take that first bold step—whether with a friend, a stranger, or a crowd—you join the unbroken line of faithful witnesses who have carried the gospel from Jerusalem to the ends of the earth. Their courage came not from themselves but from the same God Who calls you today: "Do not be afraid any longer, but go on speaking and do not be silent; for I am with you" (Acts 18:9–10).

CHAPTER 12 Building Bridges: Connecting with Skeptics and Seekers

Evangelism in the modern world requires both conviction and compassion. Many people today are skeptical of religion, distrustful of institutions, and confused about truth itself. Others are sincere seekers—searching for meaning, purpose, and spiritual reality but unsure where to find it. Both groups need the gospel, yet both require a thoughtful, patient approach. To connect with skeptics and seekers, the evangelist must not only proclaim truth but also build bridges of understanding. This work demands wisdom, humility, and love rooted firmly in Scripture. Evangelism is not about winning arguments but about guiding hearts toward the truth of God's Word.

The Challenge of a Skeptical Generation

We live in an age dominated by doubt. The rise of secularism, scientific materialism, and moral relativism has convinced many that faith is irrational or outdated. Others have been wounded by hypocrisy in religion and now reject anything labeled "Christian." This skepticism is not new; even in the first century, Paul faced philosophers who mocked the resurrection (Acts 17:32). Yet the gospel remains the same answer to the same human problem—sin and separation from God.

Skepticism, at its root, is often not intellectual but moral and spiritual. People resist belief not because the evidence is lacking, but because the implications are uncomfortable. Jesus explained, "Men loved the darkness rather than the light, for their deeds were evil" (John 3:19). Understanding this helps the evangelist to see skeptics not as enemies but as captives—ensnared by false philosophies and sin's deception.

Still, skepticism cannot be ignored or dismissed. It must be addressed with reason, patience, and grace. Building bridges with skeptics requires more than quoting Scripture; it requires understanding their worldview and gently exposing its weaknesses while pointing them to the superior truth of God's revelation.

The Heart of the Seeker

While some reject truth, others are genuinely searching for it. These seekers, though not yet believers, sense that life without God is empty. Like the Ethiopian eunuch in Acts 8:30–31, they are reading and wondering, "How can I understand unless someone guides me?" Jehovah is already at work in their hearts, drawing them toward truth through the convicting power of His Word.

The evangelist's task is to meet such seekers where they are and guide them patiently to the gospel. Seekers need clarity, not confusion; truth, not vague spirituality. They must be shown that salvation is not found through philosophy, mysticism, or good works, but through repentance and faith in Jesus Christ. When Philip met the eunuch, he "began from this Scripture and preached Jesus to him" (Acts 8:35). The same method applies today—begin with what the person understands and lead them, through Scripture, to the Savior.

The Example of Jesus: Building Bridges Without Compromise

Jesus Christ was the master bridge-builder. He met people in their context, spoke their language, and addressed their deepest needs—all while maintaining perfect fidelity to truth.

When speaking to the Samaritan woman at the well (John 4), He began with a simple request for water. This natural conversation led to spiritual truth about living water and eternal life. To Nicodemus, a religious scholar, He spoke of new birth (John 3:3). To Zacchaeus, a dishonest tax collector, He offered forgiveness and transformation (Luke 19:1–10). Jesus never compromised the message to gain acceptance; He used wisdom and love to open hearts.

Building bridges, therefore, does not mean lowering the standards of truth but finding pathways to communicate it effectively. Evangelists must imitate Christ's example: approaching people personally, speaking truth clearly, and loving them genuinely.

Understanding the Mind of the Skeptic

Skeptics often approach faith from a position of doubt shaped by experience, culture, or misinformation. To reach them, the evangelist must listen carefully before responding. Proverbs 18:13 warns, "He who gives an answer before he hears, it is folly and shame to him." Listening communicates respect and reveals the true nature of a person's objections.

Some reject the gospel because they misunderstand it. Others have intellectual questions about Scripture's reliability, the problem of evil, or the uniqueness of Christ. Still others struggle emotionally because of past pain or disappointment with religion. Understanding these distinctions allows the evangelist to respond with precision rather than generality.

Apologetics plays a vital role here. The believer must be ready "to make a defense to everyone who asks... yet with gentleness and reverence" (1 Peter 3:15). This defense involves presenting rational, historical, and moral evidence for the truth of Christianity—but always anchored in Scripture. Reason alone cannot convert, but it can remove obstacles that hinder faith. The goal is not to argue people into the Kingdom, but to clear the path so the Word of God can convict the heart.

Speaking Truth in Love

The apostle Paul instructs believers to "speak the truth in love" (Ephesians 4:15). This balance is essential when dealing with skeptics and seekers. Truth without love becomes harsh and alienating; love without truth becomes sentimental and powerless.

When engaging skeptics, truth must never be compromised to gain approval. The gospel's message of sin, judgment, and redemption cannot be softened without losing its power. Yet how truth is delivered matters. A gentle tone, patient attitude, and respectful manner can turn confrontation into conversation.

Love disarms hostility. Skeptics expect condemnation; when they encounter compassion instead, they listen. Jesus spoke firmly against sin but tenderly to sinners. The evangelist must do the same. By showing genuine care for the person behind the argument, he mirrors Christ's heart.

Finding Common Ground

Paul demonstrated remarkable skill in finding common ground with unbelievers. In Athens, he began his address by acknowledging their religious devotion: "Men of Athens, I observe that you are very religious in all respects" (Acts 17:22). From that point, he connected their altar "to an unknown god" to the truth of the one true God. He used cultural understanding as a bridge to gospel proclamation.

Likewise, modern evangelists can begin with shared human experiences—longing for purpose, morality, justice, love, or hope. These universal desires reveal the imprint of God on every heart (Romans

2:15). From these starting points, the evangelist can guide conversations toward Scripture, showing how only in Christ these longings find fulfillment.

However, finding common ground must never mean compromising conviction. Paul's bridge to the Athenians led not to philosophical discussion but to a clear declaration: "He has fixed a day in which He will judge the world in righteousness through a Man whom He has appointed, having furnished proof by raising Him from the dead" (Acts 17:31). Bridges exist to carry truth, not to dilute it.

Patience in the Process

Evangelism with skeptics and seekers is often a process, not a moment. Some will resist, others will ponder, and a few will believe immediately. The evangelist must be patient, remembering that conversion is the work of God, not man.

Paul described this divine process in 1 Corinthians 3:6: "I planted, Apollos watered, but God was causing the growth." Some believers plant seeds through initial conversations; others water through continued dialogue and prayer. But only Jehovah brings spiritual life. Impatience can lead to pressure or manipulation—neither of which produces genuine faith.

Patience also means allowing people time to wrestle with truth. Skeptics often need to unlearn years of misconceptions before they can embrace the gospel. Seekers may need time to count the cost of following Christ. The evangelist's role is to remain faithful, consistent, and prayerful, trusting God's timing.

The Role of Scripture in Building Bridges

While conversation, logic, and compassion are vital, Scripture remains the foundation of all evangelism. Only the Word of God possesses the power to convict the conscience and illuminate the heart. Hebrews 4:12 affirms that "the word of God is living and active... able to judge the thoughts and intentions of the heart."

Even skeptics who reject the Bible must hear it. The evangelist should weave Scripture naturally into dialogue, not as proof-texts but as divine truth. When people hear the Word, the Spirit of God works through it, whether they acknowledge it or not. Isaiah 55:11 promises that God's Word "will not return to Me empty, without accomplishing what I desire."

For seekers, Scripture offers clarity and assurance. When they encounter the beauty and coherence of

God's Word, their hearts often recognize its divine origin. The Bible must remain the evangelist's primary tool in every discussion.

Overcoming Barriers of Mistrust

Many modern skeptics reject Christianity not because of Christ but because of Christians. They have seen hypocrisy, pride, or abuse and concluded that religion corrupts rather than redeems. To rebuild trust, believers must model integrity, humility, and sincerity.

The evangelist must be transparent—willing to admit personal struggles while pointing to God's grace. Authenticity builds credibility. The world has seen enough hypocrisy; it longs to see holiness. When unbelievers witness genuine transformation in the believer's life, skepticism begins to crumble.

Acts of kindness also help break down barriers. When words are matched by love in action, hearts open. Jesus healed the sick, fed the hungry, and comforted the broken—all while proclaiming truth. The evangelist who demonstrates compassion while declaring Scripture reflects the Savior's heart and gains a hearing for His message.

Engaging the Intellect and the Heart

Skeptics often pride themselves on intellectual reasoning, but the gospel appeals not only to the mind but also to the heart and conscience. Paul reasoned from Scripture, but he also pleaded passionately, saying, "We beg you on behalf of Christ, be reconciled to God" (2 Corinthians 5:20).

Building bridges means addressing both intellect and emotion. Present evidence, but also share testimony. Explain truth logically, but also express it lovingly. The gospel is not merely information; it is transformation. It satisfies both the rational and relational needs of the soul.

The Importance of Prayer

Prayer is indispensable in reaching skeptics and seekers. Only Jehovah can open blind eyes and soften hardened hearts. The evangelist may present truth perfectly, but without divine intervention, the hearer remains spiritually dead.

Paul wrote, "My heart's desire and my prayer to God for them is for their salvation" (Romans 10:1). Prayer must precede, accompany, and follow every evangelistic effort. Pray for discernment to understand each person's heart, for wisdom to speak rightly, and for patience to wait on God's timing.

Prayer also protects the evangelist's own spirit from frustration and pride. It reminds him that salvation is God's work, not his own. When the believer prays for those he witnesses to, his love deepens and his dependence upon Jehovah strengthens.

The Reward of Building Bridges

Though many skeptics will resist, some will believe. Jehovah honors faithful witness. Every conversation, every question answered, and every truth spoken becomes a stepping stone toward redemption for someone.

When even one skeptic turns to Christ, Heaven rejoices (Luke 15:7). The evangelist who has patiently built bridges of truth will share in that joy. More importantly, he will have reflected the love and patience of the Savior, Who came to "seek and to save that which was lost" (Luke 19:10).

Conclusion

Building bridges with skeptics and seekers requires wisdom, humility, and perseverance. It means entering another's world not to compromise truth but to communicate it effectively. The evangelist must see skeptics not as opponents but as souls for whom Christ died, and seekers not as projects but as people in need of grace.

Through careful listening, compassionate understanding, and faithful proclamation of Scripture, believers can connect the truth of the gospel to the questions of the human heart. The goal is not to win debates but to win souls—to lead the doubting and the searching to the foot of the cross, where all questions find their ultimate answer in the person of Jesus Christ.

The bridge between unbelief and faith is built one conversation at a time, by believers who love truth and love people. May every Christian be a faithful bridge-builder, guiding skeptics and seekers from confusion to conviction, from doubt to faith, from darkness to the marvelous light of the gospel.

CHAPTER 13 Answering Objections: Equipping Yourself for Common Challenges

Evangelism often leads to encounters with honest questions—and sometimes, sharp objections. In an age of skepticism, relativism, and misinformation, Christians must not only know *what* they believe, but *why*. The Bible commands believers to "always be ready to make a defense to everyone who asks you to give an account for the hope that is in you, yet with gentleness and reverence" (1 Peter 3:15). Answering objections is not about winning debates; it is about removing barriers that prevent people from hearing the truth of God's Word.

The evangelist must be both firm in conviction and gentle in tone. Jehovah does not call His people to arrogance but to truth spoken in love. Most objections arise from ignorance, misunderstanding, or mistrust—not from reason itself. Therefore, believers must respond with clarity, wisdom, and Scripture, remembering that only God's Word has the power to convict and convert hearts (Hebrews 4:12).

Below are several common objections to the Bible and the gospel—each followed by biblically grounded responses that can equip every Christian to speak truth with confidence.

If Someone Says—"I Don't Believe in the Bible"

This objection is common among those who have never seriously examined Scripture. Many reject the Bible not because they have studied it and found it false, but because they have heard others dismiss it.

How to Respond: Ask gently, "Have you ever read it for yourself?" Most who deny the Bible's truth have not. Encourage them to begin with the Gospels—especially John—so they can encounter Christ directly. Faith comes from hearing the Word (Romans 10:17).

Then explain that belief or disbelief does not change reality. The truth of the Bible stands independently of human opinion. Just as denying gravity does not stop one from falling, denying Scripture does not nullify its truth.

Point out that the Bible's reliability is supported by overwhelming evidence. It contains sixty-six books written over fifteen centuries by more than forty authors from different cultures and backgrounds—yet it presents one unified message: Jehovah's plan of redemption through Jesus Christ. No other book in history demonstrates such consistency and preservation.

Archaeological discoveries continually confirm its historical accuracy. The Dead Sea Scrolls, for example, verify that the Old Testament we possess today is virtually identical to the one used over two thousand years ago. Moreover, the fulfillment of hundreds of detailed prophecies—such as the Messiah's birth in Bethlehem (Micah 5:2; Matthew 2:1) and His death by crucifixion (Psalm 22; John 19)—proves its divine origin.

Ultimately, belief in the Bible is not blind faith but informed trust in the evidence Jehovah has provided.

If Someone Says—"The Bible Contradicts Itself"

This objection often comes from those who have heard claims of contradictions but have not investigated them. The charge is serious because, if true, it would undermine the Bible's claim of inspiration. However, no genuine contradiction has ever been proven.

How to Respond: Explain that alleged contradictions usually arise from misunderstanding context, translation, or perspective. The Bible is a collection of writings that record different viewpoints of the same events, written by different authors for different audiences. These variations demonstrate authenticity, not error.

For example, the Gospel writers sometimes report events with differing details. One may mention two angels at the tomb, while another mentions one (compare Matthew 28:2 with John 20:12). This is not a contradiction; it is a difference in emphasis. Where there are two angels, there is at least one. The writers record complementary, not conflicting, accounts.

Apparent discrepancies often vanish when the text is studied carefully and in harmony with the whole of Scripture. As Proverbs 30:5 declares, "Every word of God is tested." The more the Bible is examined, the more its harmony shines.

The evangelist should also emphasize that critics demand perfection from Scripture while excusing far greater inconsistencies in secular history. The Bible, unlike human literature, has been scrutinized for centuries and still stands unshaken.

If Someone Says—"Men Wrote the Bible, Not God"

This objection assumes that divine revelation through human authorship is impossible. Yet the

Bible itself explains how God used men as His instruments to record His Word accurately.

How to Respond: Acknowledge that men physically wrote the Bible—but under divine guidance. The apostle Peter wrote, "No prophecy was ever made by an act of human will, but men moved by the Holy Spirit spoke from God" (2 Peter 1:21). The Greek word translated "moved" (*pheromenoi*) means "carried along," like a ship driven by the wind. The human writers expressed God's truth using their own personalities, but the content came from Him.

Paul affirmed this when he said, "All Scripture is inspired by God" (2 Timothy 3:16). The term "inspired" literally means "God-breathed." Though human hands penned the words, the breath of God gave them life.

History also confirms divine authorship. How could forty men across fifteen centuries, living in different eras and cultures, produce writings that perfectly agree on God's nature, man's sin, and the coming of the Messiah—without contradiction—unless guided by a single divine Author?

Jehovah has always chosen to work through human instruments, from the prophets of Israel to the apostles of Christ. That men wrote the Bible is not a weakness; it is evidence of God's wisdom in communicating truth to humanity in human language.

If Someone Says—"Everyone Has His Own Interpretation of the Bible"

This objection reflects the confusion of modern relativism—the belief that no single interpretation can claim to be true. But while many interpretations exist, truth itself remains singular.

How to Respond: Explain that differing interpretations do not imply the Bible is unclear, but that some readers fail to handle it properly. Peter acknowledged that certain passages are "hard to understand" and that the "untaught and unstable distort" them (2 Peter 3:16). The problem lies not with Scripture but with interpreters who approach it carelessly or with bias.

The correct approach is the *historical-grammatical method*—seeking the meaning the author intended in the historical and linguistic context. When interpreted correctly, Scripture is consistent and self-explanatory.

Moreover, Jesus expected His hearers to understand His words. He said, "Have you not read?" (Matthew 19:4), implying that Scripture's meaning can be known. The Bible's central message—God's holiness, man's sin, and salvation through Christ—is clear enough for any sincere reader to grasp.

While people may differ in secondary matters, the core truths of the gospel are unmistakable. Truth is not multiple; it is unified. Jehovah's Word is not open to private invention but demands submission to its authority.

If Someone Says—"The Bible Is Not Practical for Our Day"

Many claim that the Bible is outdated—a product of ancient culture irrelevant to modern society. Yet the Bible addresses the timeless realities of the human heart: pride, greed, lust, fear, and the longing for meaning.

How to Respond: Ask, "Has human nature changed?" Technology advances, but the moral and spiritual condition of man remains the same. The same sins that plagued humanity in the first century—violence, corruption, selfishness—fill our news headlines today. The Bible speaks directly to these issues because it speaks to the nature of man.

Scripture's moral teachings are more relevant than ever. Its call for purity, honesty, humility, and love provides the only lasting foundation for healthy families and societies. When obeyed, it transforms lives. Millions can testify that applying biblical principles has brought peace, stability, and purpose.

Furthermore, the Bible's prophecies reveal its divine foresight. It foretold the moral decline of the last days—"men will be lovers of self, lovers of money... disobedient to parents, ungrateful, unholy" (2 Timothy 3:2)—precisely describing our age. Far from being outdated, the Bible reads the modern world with astonishing accuracy.

Jehovah's Word transcends time because it comes from the eternal God. Its truth is as relevant today as when it was written.

If Someone Says—"The Bible Is a Good Book, But There Is No Such Thing as Absolute Truth"

This objection reflects the prevailing worldview of relativism, which denies objective morality and claims that truth varies by perspective. Yet such a belief contradicts itself.

How to Respond: Gently point out that to say "there is no absolute truth" is itself an absolute statement. If that statement were true, it would disprove itself. Truth, by nature, is absolute—it corresponds to reality and cannot be both true and false at the same time.

The Bible declares, "The sum of Your word is truth" (Psalm 119:160). Jesus said plainly, "Your word is truth" (John 17:17). Truth does not depend on feelings or culture; it is defined by the character of God, Who cannot lie (Titus 1:2).

Without absolute truth, moral chaos results. If good and evil are relative, justice loses meaning, and every crime can be excused. Yet even skeptics appeal to right and wrong when injustice affects them—proving that an objective moral standard exists, written on every heart (Romans 2:14–15). That standard originates not in man but in the Creator.

The Bible is not merely "a good book"; it is the revelation of absolute truth—the only solid foundation in a world built on shifting opinions.

If Someone Says—"Science Has Disproved the Bible"

This is one of the most frequent objections in the modern era, often fueled by misconceptions. True science, however, has never contradicted Scripture.

How to Respond: Clarify that science and the Bible deal with different kinds of knowledge. Science observes the natural world; the Bible reveals spiritual and moral truth. When both are rightly understood, they agree.

The Bible is not a science textbook, yet it speaks accurately whenever it touches on the natural world. Long before modern discovery, Scripture declared the earth was round (Isaiah 40:22), that it hangs "on nothing" (Job 26:7), and that the stars are countless (Jeremiah 33:22). These truths were written centuries before science confirmed them.

Many early scientists—Kepler, Newton, Pascal—believed in the God of Scripture and saw their work as studying His creation. Science explains *how* creation operates; Scripture explains *why* it exists. The Bible and science are not enemies but allies when both are interpreted properly.

The real conflict is not between science and faith, but between human pride and divine authority. The Bible calls people to repentance and submission, which many resist. Yet its truth remains unshaken by every scientific age.

If Someone Says—"Christianity Is Just One of Many Religions"

This objection assumes all religions are equally valid, yet their teachings fundamentally contradict one another.

How to Respond: Explain that truth, by definition, excludes what contradicts it. If Christianity is true, then other religions that deny Christ's deity or resurrection cannot also be true. Jesus claimed exclusivity: "I am the way, and the truth, and the life; no one comes to the Father but through Me" (John 14:6).

Unlike other religions, Christianity is not based on human philosophy or moral effort but on a historical event—the resurrection of Jesus Christ. The empty tomb is an undeniable fact, attested by eyewitnesses willing to die for their testimony. No other religion offers verifiable evidence of its founder's triumph over death.

While all religions express humanity's search for God, Christianity is about God's search for humanity through His Son. This distinction makes it not one of many paths, but the only path established by God Himself.

If Someone Says—"There Is Too Much Evil in the World for There to Be a God"

The presence of evil troubles many, yet the Bible offers the only coherent explanation and solution.

How to Respond: Acknowledge the pain behind the question. Evil and suffering are real and grievous. However, the existence of evil does not disprove God—it proves humanity's rebellion against Him. Jehovah created the world good (Genesis 1:31). Evil entered through man's disobedience (Genesis 3). Since then, sin has corrupted creation, causing pain, injustice, and death.

But God did not remain distant. He entered the world through Christ to defeat evil through the cross. The crucifixion shows that God is not indifferent to suffering; He bore it Himself. Through Jesus' resurrection, He guarantees a future where evil and death will be no more (Revelation 21:4).

The atheist still faces the same problem of evil without a solution. Without God, there is no objective standard by which to call anything evil. Only Christianity both explains evil's origin and promises its ultimate removal.

Developing the Right Attitude When Answering Objections

The manner of response is as important as the content. Paul instructed Timothy to correct opponents "with gentleness, if perhaps God may grant them repentance leading to the knowledge of the truth" (2 Timothy 2:25). The goal is not intellectual victory but spiritual restoration.

Be humble—remember that you, too, once needed God's grace. Be patient—many objections mask deeper struggles or emotional wounds. Be prayerful—only the Spirit working through the Word can open blind eyes.

Every objection is an opportunity to share the truth of Jehovah's Word and display the love of Christ. Some hearts will resist; others will soften over time. Faithfulness, not argument, is what God requires.

Conclusion

Answering objections requires more than knowledge—it requires faith, wisdom, and love. Skeptics and seekers raise many challenges, but none that the truth of Scripture cannot meet. The Bible has withstood centuries of scrutiny, and its light continues to pierce the darkness of unbelief.

When you stand upon God's Word, you stand on unshakable ground. You need not fear objections; you only need to be faithful to the truth. Speak with gentleness and conviction, showing that Christianity is not blind faith but rational, historical, and moral truth revealed by the living God.

In every question, point people back to Scripture—for there, and only there, lies the answer that satisfies the mind and transforms the heart.

CHAPTER 14 Evangelizing Like Jesus Christ

To evangelize like Jesus Christ is to follow the perfect example of the Master Evangelist. No one proclaimed truth with greater clarity, compassion, and authority than He. His words transformed lives, His manner revealed grace and truth, and His mission defined the very purpose of evangelism itself. Every Christian who desires to share the gospel faithfully must study not only what Jesus taught, but how He reached people. The Gospels provide not just doctrine but demonstration—the divine model of how to proclaim the good news effectively.

Evangelizing like Jesus means aligning one's message, method, and motive with His. It means seeing people as He saw them, loving them as He loved them, and speaking with both courage and compassion. Christ's ministry shows that evangelism is not a program but a way of life—a continual outpouring of truth motivated by love for God and others.

The Mission of Jesus: To Seek and to Save

Jesus defined His mission with absolute clarity: "For the Son of Man has come to seek and to save that which was lost" (Luke 19:10). Evangelism was not a side task or a secondary concern—it was His central purpose. Every conversation, miracle, and parable pointed toward that goal. His mission was redemptive, and His entire life was an act of evangelism.

He saw humanity not as statistics or crowds but as individuals in need of salvation. His heart moved with compassion whenever He saw people "distressed and dispirited like sheep without a shepherd" (Matthew 9:36). The same compassion must drive every believer's evangelism. We do not evangelize to fulfill obligation but because we share the Savior's heart for the lost.

To evangelize like Jesus, therefore, begins with adopting His purpose. The believer must see himself as a co-laborer in the same mission—to seek the lost through truth and love. Every Christian is called to reflect Christ's redemptive heart in daily life, turning ordinary moments into opportunities for salvation.

The Message of Jesus: Repent and Believe the Gospel

Jesus' message was consistent and uncompromising. From the beginning of His ministry, He proclaimed, "Repent, for the kingdom of heaven is at hand" (Matthew 4:17). His gospel called for personal repentance and faith in Him as the Messiah and Son of God.

He did not water down the truth to please audiences or avoid controversy. He confronted sin directly yet tenderly, offering forgiveness to the repentant and warning of judgment to the unrepentant. His message revealed the holiness of God, the sinfulness of man, and the necessity of reconciliation through faith.

To evangelize like Jesus means proclaiming the same gospel with the same seriousness. The evangelist must resist the temptation to replace the message of repentance and faith with vague moralism or emotional appeal. Jesus never told people merely to "be better"; He told them to be born again (John 3:3).

Modern evangelism often seeks to attract through entertainment or ease. But Jesus presented the gospel as both invitation and confrontation. He offered life, yet demanded surrender. He said, "If anyone wishes to come after Me, he must deny himself, and take up his cross and follow Me" (Matthew 16:24). Evangelizing like Christ requires that we restore this biblical balance—grace that saves and truth that transforms.

The Method of Jesus: Personal, Purposeful, and Penetrating

Jesus did not confine His ministry to public preaching. He met individuals where they were, addressing their unique needs and questions. His evangelism was deeply personal, never mechanical.

When He spoke to Nicodemus, He discussed new birth. With the Samaritan woman, He spoke of living water. With the rich young ruler, He addressed misplaced priorities. With the woman caught in adultery, He offered forgiveness and a call to holiness. Jesus never used a "one-size-fits-all" approach; He met people's hearts with divine precision.

Evangelizing like Jesus requires sensitivity and discernment. The believer must learn to listen, observe, and apply truth appropriately. Jesus' conversations were not random; they were purposeful. He guided each one toward the ultimate question of faith: "Who do you say that I am?" (Matthew 16:15).

His words penetrated beyond surface issues to expose the heart. He revealed sin not to shame but to save. The evangelist who imitates Christ must likewise aim beyond outward behavior to the inward need for redemption. Evangelism is not persuasion by logic alone, but illumination by truth through Scripture.

The Compassion of Jesus: Love That Breaks Barriers

Jesus' evangelism was rooted in love that broke social, religious, and cultural barriers. He spoke with Samaritans whom Jews despised, touched lepers whom society rejected, and showed mercy to sinners whom religion condemned. His outreach defied prejudice and revealed that the gospel is for all people.

In John 4, His encounter with the Samaritan woman demonstrates this perfectly. Despite cultural taboos, He initiated conversation, revealed her spiritual need, and offered eternal life. He did not condemn her past but invited her into transformation. As a result, she became one of the first witnesses in her town.

To evangelize like Jesus means loving people regardless of their background, status, or sin. The gospel knows no boundaries. Every soul is precious to God, and every believer is called to show that same inclusive compassion. Evangelism without love becomes cold argument; evangelism with love reflects the heart of Christ.

Paul echoed this principle when he said, "The love of Christ controls us" (2 Corinthians 5:14). Love gives courage to speak, patience to listen, and grace to forgive. Without it, evangelism loses its power.

The Authority of Jesus: Speaking the Word of God

Jesus' authority amazed His listeners. "He was teaching them as one having authority, and not as their scribes" (Matthew 7:29). His authority did not come from human approval but from divine truth. Every word He spoke carried the full weight of Scripture.

He constantly quoted the Old Testament, saying, "It is written." He used Scripture to confront temptation (Matthew 4:4), correct misunderstanding (Matthew 22:29), and affirm His mission (Luke 4:21). His evangelism was inseparable from the Word of God.

To evangelize like Jesus, believers must anchor every conversation in Scripture. Personal testimony and reasoning are helpful, but only the Word has divine authority. Hebrews 4:12 describes it as "living and active... able to judge the thoughts and intentions of the heart." When we proclaim the gospel, we must let Scripture speak for itself.

Jesus demonstrated that truth does not need embellishment—it needs proclamation. Evangelists must therefore speak with the same confidence, knowing they bear the message of the King. The authority lies not in tone or personality but in the inspired Word they declare.

The Simplicity of Jesus' Evangelism

Though profound in meaning, Jesus' message was simple in expression. He used everyday language and familiar illustrations—seeds, sheep, lamps, bread, and water—to explain spiritual truth. He did not confuse with complexity; He clarified with simplicity.

This simplicity made His message accessible to the common person. The crowds "heard Him gladly" (Mark 12:37). Even children could understand His teaching. Yet beneath this simplicity lay eternal depth. His parables concealed profound truths that both revealed and tested hearts.

To evangelize like Jesus means communicating clearly. The gospel must not be obscured by academic jargon or emotional manipulation. Speak plainly of sin, salvation, faith, and forgiveness. Jesus taught that the truth itself is powerful enough to convict. Our task is not to impress, but to express the gospel faithfully.

The Courage of Jesus: Truth Without Compromise

Jesus was compassionate, yet never compromising. His love did not dilute His message. He confronted hypocrisy in the religious elite, saying, "Woe to you, scribes and Pharisees, hypocrites!" (Matthew 23:13). He warned of Hell (Matthew 10:28) and called for repentance (Luke 13:3). His evangelism was both tender and terrifying—grace for the humble and judgment for the proud.

To evangelize like Jesus means being fearless in declaring truth, regardless of reaction. Many turned away from Him when His words became too demanding (John 6:66), yet He did not soften His message. The evangelist must resist the temptation to please men. Faithfulness to truth must outweigh fear of rejection.

Courage is not harshness; it is loyalty to God. The true evangelist, like his Master, must be willing to stand alone if necessary. The cost of truth is often rejection, but the reward is obedience to Christ.

The Prayer Life of Jesus: Dependence on the Father

Before every major act of ministry, Jesus prayed. Before choosing the twelve apostles, "He spent the whole night in prayer to God" (Luke 6:12). Before preaching, healing, or facing the cross, He sought communion with His Father. His evangelistic power flowed from prayerful dependence.

If the sinless Son of God relied upon prayer, how much more must His followers? Evangelism without prayer is powerless. Prayer aligns the evangelist's heart with God's will, opens doors of opportunity, and prepares hearts to receive truth. Paul understood this and asked believers to pray "that God will open up to us a door for the word" (Colossians 4:3).

To evangelize like Jesus is to evangelize prayerfully. Begin every outreach with prayer, intercede for those who hear, and thank God for every response. Prayer fuels boldness, deepens compassion, and sustains perseverance.

The Discipleship of Jesus: Evangelism That Multiplies

Jesus did not merely make converts; He made disciples. His evangelism always aimed toward transformation and multiplication. He called individuals not just to believe, but to follow. "Follow Me, and I will make you fishers of men" (Matthew 4:19).

He invested deeply in His disciples, teaching them to carry on His mission. He modeled ministry, explained truth, corrected errors, and commissioned them to continue His work. By focusing on a few, He reached the many.

To evangelize like Jesus means thinking beyond immediate results. True evangelism includes nurturing new believers, grounding them in Scripture, and equipping them to evangelize others. The Great Commission is not only to make disciples but to teach them "to observe all that I commanded you" (Matthew 28:20).

Evangelism that stops at conversion falls short of Christ's pattern. Evangelism that reproduces disciples continues His mission through generations.

The Compassionate Urgency of Jesus

Jesus' evangelism was urgent. He knew that every soul stood on the brink of eternity. He warned of judgment and pleaded for repentance, yet always with compassion. "We must work the works of Him who sent Me as long as it is day; night is coming when no one can work" (John 9:4).

He wasted no opportunity. Whether speaking to multitudes or to one sinner, He acted with the awareness that time was short. The evangelist must carry this same urgency—not panic, but passion. The opportunity to speak today may never come again.

To evangelize like Jesus means to live with eternity in view, recognizing that every person will one day stand before God. Love compels urgency; complacency betrays indifference.

The Results of Jesus' Evangelism

Not everyone who heard Jesus believed. Some followed Him gladly; others mocked or rejected Him. Yet His mission was fulfilled because He faithfully proclaimed the Father's Word. Evangelistic success is measured not by response but by obedience.

The same principle applies to believers today. Some will receive the message with joy; others will resist. The evangelist's duty is to sow faithfully, trusting God for the increase (1 Corinthians 3:6). Jesus prepared His disciples for this reality, saying that the seed of the Word falls on different kinds of soil (Matthew 13:3–23).

To evangelize like Jesus is to remain steadfast regardless of outcome. Faithfulness brings peace, for the results belong to Jehovah alone.

Conclusion

Evangelizing like Jesus Christ means more than repeating His words—it means imitating His heart, His holiness, and His humility. He taught truth boldly, loved sinners deeply, prayed continually, and lived righteously. His life was a message as much as His words.

The believer who seeks to evangelize as Jesus did must follow the same path: anchored in Scripture, motivated by love, dependent on prayer, fearless in truth, and devoted to making disciples. This is not merely a method—it is a way of life that reflects the Savior Himself.

Jesus' example transforms evangelism from a task into a calling, from an obligation into a joy. When Christians learn to see people as He did and speak truth as He spoke it, they continue His mission on earth. The greatest compliment to a believer's witness is to be recognized as one who evangelizes like Christ—faithful to truth, rich in mercy, and filled with the love of God.

CHAPTER 15 Evangelizing Like the Apostle Paul: Reasoning, Explaining, Proving, and Persuading with the Gospel

Among all the evangelists of Scripture, the Apostle Paul stands as the greatest model of intellectual clarity, doctrinal precision, and unwavering zeal for the truth. If Jesus Christ is the divine pattern of evangelism, Paul is the human example of how to apply that pattern in real-world ministry. His bold preaching turned the Roman Empire upside down. His logical reasoning silenced opponents. His compassionate persuasion won multitudes to Christ. And his written letters—preserved by divine inspiration—continue to equip believers to proclaim the gospel with conviction and confidence.

Paul's evangelistic method was never casual or shallow. He did not rely on emotional manipulation or cultural conformity. He used the power of truth, reason, and persuasion grounded in Scripture. Acts describes his consistent pattern of evangelism: "He reasoned with them from the Scriptures, explaining and giving evidence that the Christ had to suffer and rise again from the dead, and saying, 'This Jesus whom I am proclaiming to you is the Christ'" (Acts 17:2–3).

Those five verbs—*reasoned*, *explained*, *gave evidence*, *proclaimed*, and *persuaded*—summarize the apostolic approach to evangelism. Every faithful Christian should learn to follow Paul's example, combining sound doctrine with deep compassion, intellectual strength with spiritual humility.

The Foundation of Paul's Evangelism: Conviction in the Gospel

Paul's ministry began and ended with the same conviction: that the gospel is the power of God for salvation. He declared boldly, "I am not ashamed of the gospel, for it is the power of God for salvation to everyone who believes" (Romans 1:16).

This conviction shaped his entire approach to evangelism. Paul believed that salvation does not come through human wisdom, emotional appeal, or philosophical debate, but through the proclamation of God's revealed truth. His confidence was not in himself but in the Word. He understood that the message, not the messenger, carries divine power.

To evangelize like Paul, the believer must begin with this same unshakable confidence in the sufficiency of Scripture. Every conversation, sermon, or defense must be anchored in the conviction that Jehovah's Word alone transforms hearts. Evangelism loses power when it departs from this foundation.

Paul Reasoned from the Scriptures

The book of Acts repeatedly emphasizes Paul's use of reasoning. In Thessalonica, "he reasoned with them from the Scriptures" (Acts 17:2). In Corinth, "he was reasoning in the synagogue every Sabbath and trying to persuade Jews and Greeks" (Acts 18:4). In Ephesus, "he entered the synagogue and continued speaking out boldly for three months, reasoning and persuading them about the kingdom of God" (Acts 19:8).

The Greek word for "reasoned" (*dialegomai*) means to dialogue or to engage in discussion. Paul did not merely preach at people; he conversed with them. He listened, responded, and guided them toward truth. His reasoning was logical yet Spirit-led, always rooted in Scripture.

For Paul, reasoning was not an academic exercise but a spiritual weapon. He wrote, "We are destroying speculations and every lofty thing raised up against the knowledge of God" (2 Corinthians 10:5). He confronted false beliefs not with hostility but with reasoned truth.

To evangelize like Paul, Christians must learn to think biblically and reason clearly. Evangelism involves explaining why the gospel is true and demonstrating how it answers the deepest questions of life. Faith is not irrational; it is reasonable because it rests on the revelation of the Creator.

Paul Explained the Truth Clearly

Paul was a master teacher. He knew that truth must be explained before it can be embraced. Luke records that he was "explaining and giving evidence that the Christ had to suffer and rise again" (Acts 17:3).

The word *explaining* means to open or make plain. Paul unfolded Scripture like a skilled expositor, showing the logical progression of prophecy and fulfillment. He connected the dots between the Old Testament promises and the New Testament realities. He demonstrated that the suffering Messiah of Isaiah 53 was the crucified and risen Jesus of Nazareth.

Paul's explanations were neither vague nor emotional. They were clear, sequential, and supported by Scripture. His hearers could follow his reasoning from premise to conclusion. He made truth understandable.

Believers today must follow this example. Evangelism is not merely proclaiming slogans but clearly explaining biblical truth—what sin is, who Jesus is, why He died, and how faith brings forgiveness. The message must be coherent, not confusing; scriptural, not superficial.

Paul's clarity came from his mastery of the Word. To evangelize like him, Christians must study deeply, so they can explain accurately. Evangelistic zeal without knowledge leads to error, but knowledge with zeal leads to transformation.

Paul Proved the Gospel with Evidence

Luke also notes that Paul was "giving evidence" that the Christ had to suffer and rise again (Acts 17:3). The word *proving* (KJV) or *giving evidence* (NASB) means to set before or demonstrate logically. Paul did not expect blind faith; he provided rational, historical, and prophetic evidence to show that Jesus was the promised Messiah.

His evidence included fulfilled prophecy, eyewitness testimony, the reality of the resurrection, and the moral transformation of believers. When speaking to Jews, he showed from the Scriptures how the prophecies of the Messiah's suffering were fulfilled in Jesus (Isaiah 53; Psalm 22). When addressing Gentiles, he appealed to natural revelation—the Creator revealed in the world around them (Acts 17:24–27).

Paul's evidential approach demonstrates that faith and reason are not enemies. Christianity invites investigation. The resurrection, the cornerstone of the gospel, rests on historical fact. Paul boldly stated that Christ "appeared to more than five hundred brethren at one time... most of whom remain until now" (1 Corinthians 15:6). He invited verification, not blind acceptance.

To evangelize like Paul, Christians must be prepared to *prove* their message—not by personal opinion, but by Scripture, reason, and historical fact. The gospel is not an emotional idea; it is a rational reality backed by evidence.

Paul Persuaded with Passion

Above all, Paul was a persuader. His goal was not mere discussion but conviction leading to faith. Acts 18:4 records that he "reasoned in the synagogue every Sabbath and tried to persuade Jews and Greeks." His method combined logic and passion, intellect and compassion.

The word *persuade* means to convince through reasoned appeal. Paul's aim was not to win arguments but to win souls. His persuasion was marked by sincerity, urgency, and love. He did not manipulate; he pleaded. "Therefore, knowing the fear of the Lord, we persuade men" (2 Corinthians 5:11).

True persuasion requires personal conviction. Paul believed what he preached with his entire being. His message was not theoretical; it was personal. He had encountered the risen Christ, and that reality consumed his life. Every word he spoke came from deep gratitude and zeal for the glory of God.

To evangelize like Paul is to combine truth with love, logic with compassion, and confidence with humility. Persuasion requires empathy. The evangelist must understand the listener's doubts, fears, and worldview, addressing each with patient truth.

Paul persuaded both scholars and commoners, Jews and Gentiles, rich and poor. Whether speaking before philosophers in Athens (Acts 17) or prisoners in Philippi (Acts 16), he adapted his approach without compromising the message. He was, as he said, "all things to all men, so that I may by all means save some" (1 Corinthians 9:22).

Paul's Intellectual Evangelism

Paul's education and background made him uniquely suited for intellectual evangelism. Trained under Gamaliel, familiar with Greek philosophy, and fluent in multiple languages, he used his knowledge to engage both Jewish and Gentile audiences. Yet he never relied on intellect alone. He reminded the Corinthians that his message was "not in persuasive words of wisdom, but in demonstration of the Spirit and of power" (1 Corinthians 2:4).

He valued logic, but he depended on the Spirit. His reasoning opened minds, but God's power opened hearts. This balance is essential. Evangelists must use every faculty of the mind while relying entirely on the Spirit's work through Scripture.

Paul's intellectual depth gave credibility to his message in a world steeped in skepticism. He challenged idolatry in Athens, materialism in Corinth, and legalism in Galatia. His arguments were sharp but gracious, firm but fair. He met unbelief head-on with unshakable truth.

Paul's Scriptural Foundation

Paul's entire evangelistic method rested on the Scriptures. His reasoning, explaining, proving, and persuading all flowed from the authority of God's Word. He did not invent ideas but revealed what was already written.

In Romans 10:17 he summarized his theology of evangelism: "Faith comes from hearing, and hearing by the word of Christ." Without Scripture, there is no faith, for the Spirit works only through the inspired Word.

Paul's sermons in Acts consistently begin with Scripture. In Acts 13, addressing Jews in Pisidian Antioch, he reviewed Israel's history to show that Jesus fulfilled the promises to David. In Acts 17, he used creation and conscience to reach pagan Greeks but still pointed them back to the Creator revealed in Scripture. In every setting, his message was biblical, not speculative.

To evangelize like Paul, one must love and know the Scriptures deeply. The Bible must be both the foundation and the content of every evangelistic conversation.

Paul's Emotional and Spiritual Passion

Paul's intellect never overshadowed his heart. He wrote to the Romans, "My heart's desire and my prayer to God for them is for their salvation" (Romans 10:1). Evangelism, for Paul, was not mere duty—it was the outflow of love for God and people.

He described his ministry with tears: "Remember that night and day for a period of three years I did not cease to admonish each one with tears" (Acts 20:31). He wept for the lost, prayed for the unconverted, and rejoiced over every repentant soul.

This combination of truth and tenderness made his evangelism powerful. He knew that reasoning alone could not change hearts, but love could open doors for truth. To evangelize like Paul means to care deeply about the eternal destiny of others.

Paul's Adaptability Without Compromise

Paul's method changed according to his audience, but his message never did. To Jews, he appealed to Scripture; to Gentiles, he began with creation. He contextualized without compromising.

In Acts 17, standing among Greek philosophers, he quoted their poets to build rapport before declaring, "What you worship in ignorance, this I proclaim to you" (Acts 17:23). He began with their worldview but ended with the gospel.

This adaptability reflects strategic wisdom. The evangelist must know his audience—their beliefs, doubts, and influences—so he can build bridges to biblical truth. Yet those bridges must always lead to the same destination: repentance and faith in Christ.

To evangelize like Paul is to understand the times without being shaped by them, to engage culture without conforming to it.

Paul's Perseverance Amid Opposition

Paul faced constant hostility—imprisonment, ridicule, stoning, and persecution—but he never stopped proclaiming Christ. In Lystra, after being stoned and left for dead, he rose and went back into the city to continue preaching (Acts 14:19–20).

His courage came from his confidence in God's sovereignty. "We do not lose heart," he wrote, "for we have this treasure in earthen vessels, so that the surpassing greatness of the power will be of God and not from ourselves" (2 Corinthians 4:1, 7).

Evangelizing like Paul requires endurance. Opposition should be expected, not feared. The gospel challenges pride, confronts sin, and exposes falsehood; therefore, resistance is inevitable. But the evangelist who trusts God's power will remain steadfast.

The Persuasive Power of Paul's Example

Paul's life validated his message. His transformed character was living proof of the gospel's power. Once a persecutor of Christians, he became their greatest preacher. His testimony of grace gave credibility to his words.

In Galatians 1:23, the believers marveled, saying, "He who once persecuted us is now preaching the faith which he once tried to destroy." His life was the evidence that Christ changes hearts.

To evangelize like Paul means to live consistently with the message we proclaim. Integrity amplifies truth; hypocrisy silences it. The evangelist's life must display the transformation he urges others to experience.

Conclusion

Evangelizing like the Apostle Paul means reasoning clearly, explaining faithfully, proving convincingly, and persuading compassionately. His example demonstrates that effective evangelism is both intellectual and spiritual, rational and relational, courageous and compassionate.

Paul's method was not shallow appeal but deep conviction; not manipulation, but persuasion grounded in truth. He reasoned from Scripture, explained the gospel's necessity, proved its truth with evidence, and persuaded with passion. He adapted his approach to each audience while remaining faithful to the message.

Above all, Paul evangelized with a heart burning for the glory of Christ. He was tireless, fearless, and faithful because he believed that eternity was at stake. His cry to the Corinthians echoes through the centuries: "Woe is me if I do not preach the gospel!" (1 Corinthians 9:16).

Every believer who seeks to evangelize like Paul must embrace the same conviction—that the gospel is the power of God for salvation, that truth can withstand scrutiny, and that love must motivate every word spoken. When Christians reason, explain, prove, and persuade with the heart of Paul and the truth of

Christ, the world will again see the transforming power of God through the gospel.

Glossary of Terms

Absolute Truth – The belief that truth is objective, universal, and grounded in the nature of God, not subject to human opinion or cultural perspective.

Ad Hominem – A logical fallacy in which an argument attacks the person making a claim rather than addressing the claim itself.

Ambassador for Christ – A title for believers representing Christ to the world through proclamation, conduct, and defense of the gospel (2 Corinthians 5:20).

Apologia (Greek) – Meaning "defense" or "reasoned statement," the biblical term that forms the basis for *apologetics* (1 Peter 3:15).

Apologetics – The reasoned defense and confirmation of the Christian faith, demonstrating its truth, rationality, and coherence with reality.

Apostasy – The act of abandoning or rejecting the faith once professed; often associated with false teaching and moral compromise.

Atheism – The worldview that denies the existence of God; refuted in the book as irrational and self-defeating since it cannot justify truth, morality, or reason.

Authority of Scripture – The teaching that the Bible is the ultimate and final standard for truth, doctrine, and moral conduct.

Biblical Apologetics (Presuppositional) – A branch of apologetics that begins with the authority of Scripture, showing that all reasoning presupposes God's revelation.

Christocentric – Having Christ as the center and focus of faith, theology, and evangelism.

Classical Apologetics – A two-step apologetic approach that first demonstrates the existence of God through reason and evidence, then confirms Christianity as true through historical and biblical proof.

Common Grace – God's benevolence shown to all humanity through creation and conscience, even apart from saving faith.

Conversion – The turning of a person from sin to faith in Christ, resulting in regeneration and reconciliation with God.

Cultural Discernment – The ability to recognize and evaluate cultural ideas and practices according to biblical truth.

Deism – The belief in a distant Creator who does not intervene in human affairs; rejected as inconsistent with biblical revelation.

Discipleship – The process of spiritual growth and obedience to Christ following conversion; the ultimate goal of evangelism.

Empirical Evidence – Observable and verifiable data used in evidential apologetics to demonstrate the reliability of Scripture and the historical truth of Christ's resurrection.

Epistemology – The study of knowledge and belief; Christian epistemology asserts that true knowledge begins with "the fear of Jehovah" (Proverbs 1:7).

Eschatology – The study of end times, including Christ's return and the final judgment; the book affirms premillennial eschatology.

Evidential Apologetics – An approach that uses historical and empirical evidence (such as fulfilled prophecy, miracles, and the resurrection) to confirm the truth of Christianity.

Evangelism – The proclamation of the gospel message of salvation through Jesus Christ, calling people to repentance and faith.

Faith – Rational trust in God and His Word, grounded in evidence and revelation rather than blind belief.

Fallacy – A flaw in reasoning that weakens an argument; apologists are warned to avoid these in defending the faith.

General Revelation – God's self-disclosure through nature, conscience, and history, making His existence evident to all people (Romans 1:20).

Gentleness and Respect – The biblical manner required of all apologists (1 Peter 3:15); truth must be spoken in love.

Gospel – The good news of salvation through the life, death, and resurrection of Jesus Christ.

Grace – God's unmerited favor given to humanity for salvation and sanctification.

Heretic / Heresy – A person or teaching that contradicts essential biblical truths; apologetics guards the church against heresy.

Historical-Grammatical Method – The proper method of interpreting Scripture by examining its original grammar, context, and authorial intent to discern literal meaning.

Holiness – Moral and spiritual purity reflecting God's character; essential to the credibility of the evangelist and apologist.

Illumination – The work of God's Spirit through Scripture that enables understanding of divine truth.

Imago Dei – Latin for "Image of God"; the biblical teaching that humanity was created to reflect God's nature and moral capacity (Genesis 1:26–27).

Inerrancy – The doctrine that Scripture is without error in all that it affirms in its original manuscripts.

Jehovah – The personal covenant name of God used throughout the book to reflect His self-revelation as the one true God.

Justification – The divine act of declaring a sinner righteous through faith in Christ alone.

Logic – The study of correct reasoning; used in apologetics to demonstrate the coherence of the Christian worldview.

Lordship of Christ – The recognition that Jesus Christ is sovereign over all areas of life, including thought, morality, and truth.

Miracle – A supernatural act of God that confirms divine truth and validates the message or messenger (e.g., Jesus' resurrection).

Monotheism – The belief in one true God; foundational to Christian theism.

Natural Revelation – Another term for general revelation—God's witness through the created order.

Objective Morality – The belief that moral truths are absolute and grounded in God's nature, not human preference.

Orthodox Christianity – The body of essential Christian doctrine consistent with the teachings of Scripture and the apostles.

Pauline Persuasion – The method of persuasion used by the Apostle Paul, combining logical reasoning (*peithō*) with spiritual conviction and compassion.

Peithō (Greek) – The verb meaning "to persuade" or "to convince," used by Paul to describe his evangelistic reasoning.

Philosophical Apologetics – The branch of apologetics dealing with ultimate questions of existence, truth, and morality through rational argumentation.

Presuppositional Apologetics – The apologetic approach that begins with the presupposition that Scripture is the ultimate authority for truth and reason.

Prophecy – Divine revelation of future events, often cited in apologetics as evidence for the Bible's inspiration and the Messiahship of Jesus.

Rational Faith – Belief that harmonizes with evidence, reason, and Scripture.

Reconciliation – The restoration of fellowship between God and man through the atoning work of Christ.

Redemption – The act of being delivered from sin's penalty and power through Christ's sacrifice.

Regeneration – The new birth wrought by God, producing spiritual life in those who believe in Christ.

Relativism – The belief that truth and morality are subjective and culturally defined; refuted throughout the book as logically self-defeating.

Repentance – A turning from sin to God in genuine sorrow and obedience.

Revelation (Divine) – God's act of making Himself known through creation (general revelation) and Scripture (special revelation).

Sanctification – The process by which believers are made holy and conformed to the image of Christ.

Scripture Sufficiency – The teaching that the Bible contains all truth necessary for salvation, faith, and obedience.

Sin – Rebellion against God and violation of His moral law; the universal human problem requiring redemption.

Soteriology – The doctrine of salvation, encompassing justification, regeneration, and sanctification.

Special Revelation – God's specific self-disclosure through His Word and through Jesus Christ.

Theism – The belief in a personal, infinite, and moral Creator who is active in His creation; contrasted with atheism, deism, and pantheism.

Trinity – The biblical doctrine that the one God eternally exists in three distinct persons: Father, Son, and Holy Spirit.

Truth – That which corresponds to reality and is consistent with God's character and revelation.

Witness – The act of testifying to the truth of Christ through word and deed.

Worldview – The comprehensive framework of beliefs through which one interprets reality; the

Christian worldview alone is consistent, moral, and true.

Worship – Reverent devotion and obedience to God in all areas of life; evangelism and apologetics are forms of worship when done for His glory.

Bibliography

Andrews, E. D. (2012). *DIFFICULTIES IN THE BIBLE UPDATED: Updated and Expanded.* Cambridge, OH: Christian Publishing House.

Andrews, E. D. (2016). *INTERPRETING THE BIBLE: Introduction to Biblical Hermeneutics.* Cambridge, OH: Christian Publishing House.

Andrews, E. D. (2016). *THE COMPLETE GUIDE to BIBLE TRANSLATION: Bible Translation Choices and Translation Principles [Second Edition] .* Cambridge: Christian Publishing House.

Andrews, E. D. (2016). *THE EVANGELISM HANDBOOK: How All Christians Can Effectively Share God's Word in Their Community, [SECOND EDITION].* Cambridge, OH: Christian Publishing House.

Andrews, E. D. (2016). *YOUR GUIDE FOR DEFENDING THE BIBLE: Self-Education of the Bible Made Easy.* Cambridge, OH: Christian Publishing House.

Andrews, E. D. (2017). *CONVERSATIONAL EVANGELISM: Defending the Faith,*

Reasoning from the Scriptures, Explaining and Proving, Instructing in Sound Doctrine, and Overturning False Reasoning [Second Edition]. Cambridge, OH: Christian Publishing House.

Andrews, E. D. (2017). *IS THE BIBLE REALLY THE WORD OF GOD?: Is Christianity the One True Faith?* Cambridge, Ohio: Christian Publishing House.

Andrews, E. D. (2017). *IS THE QURAN THE WORD OF GOD?: Is Islam the One True Faith.* Cambridge, OH: Christian Publishing House.

Andrews, E. D. (2018). *CHRISTIAN APOLOGETIC EVANGELISM: Reaching Hearts with the Art of Persuasion.* Cambridge, OH: Christian Publishing House.

Andrews, E. D. (2018). *REASONING WITH THE WORLD'S VARIOUS RELIGIONS: Examining and Evangelizing Other Faiths.* Cambridge, OH: Christian Publishing House.

Andrews, E. D. (2018). *The CHURCH CURE: Overcoming Church Problems.* Cambridge, OH: Christian Publishing House.

Andrews, E. D. (2019). *MIRACLES: What Does the Bible Really Teach?* Cambridge, OH: Christian Publishing House.

Andrews, E. D. (2022). *THE QUEST FOR THE HISTORICAL JESUS: Are Doubts About Jesus Justified?* Cambridge, OH: Christian Publishing House.

Andrews, E. D. (2023). *BIBLICAL EXEGESIS: Biblical Criticism on Trial.* Cambridge, OH: Christian Publishing House.

Andrews, E. D. (2023). *CHRISTIAN APOLOGETICS: Answering the Tough Questions: Evidence and Reason in Defense of the Faith.* Cambridge, Ohio: Christian Publishing House.

Andrews, E. D. (2023). *HOW WE GOT THE BIBLE.* Cambridge, OH: Christian Publishing House.

Andrews, E. D. (2023). *ISLAM & THE QURAN: Examining the Quran & Islamic Teachings.* Cambridge, OH: Christian Publishing House.

Andrews, E. D. (2023). *ISLAMIC ESCHATOLOGY: Awaiting Al-Mahdi—The Twelfth Imam and the Future of Islam.* Cambridge, OH: Christian Publishing House.

Andrews, E. D. (2023). *THE BIBLE ON TRIAL: Examining the Evidence for Being Inspired, Inerrant, Authentic, and True.* Cambridge, Ohio: Christian Publishing House.

Andrews, E. D. (2023). *UNSHAKABLE BELIEFS: Strategies for Strengthening and Defending Your Faith.* Cambridge, OH: Christian Publishing House.

Andrews, E. D. (2024). *BATTLE PLANS: A Game Plan for Answering Objections to the Christian Faith.* Cambridge, OH: Christian Publishing House.

Andrews, E. D. (2024). *CREATION AND COSMOS: A Journey Through Creation, Science, and the Origins of Life.* Cambridge, OH: Christian Publishing House.

Andrews, E. D. (2024). *FAITH UNDER FIRE: Refuting the Top 30 Arguments Atheists Make Against Christianity.* Cambridge, OH: Christian Publishing House.

Andrews, E. D. (2024). *REASON MEETS FAITH: Addressing and Refuting Atheism's Challenges to Christianity.* Cambridge, OH: Christian Publishing House.

Andrews, E. D. (2024). *THE ENCYCLOPEDIA OF CHRISTIAN APOLOGETICS: The Resource for Pastors, Teachers, and Believers.* Cambridge: Christan Publishing House.

Andrews, E. D. (2024). *THE HISTORICAL ADAM & EVE: Reconciling Faith and Fact in Genesis.* Cambridge, OH: Christian Publishing House.

Andrews, E. D. (2024). *THE HISTORICAL JESUS: The Death, Burial, and Resurrection of Jesus Christ.* Cambridge, OH: Christian Publishing House.

Andrews, E. D. (2025). *ATHEISM: What Will You Say to an Atheist.* Cambridge, OH: Christian Publising House.

Andrews, E. D. (2025). *BIBLE DIFFICULTIES: How to Approach Difficulties In the Bible.* Cambridge, OH: Christian Publishing House.

Andrews, E. D. (2025). *BIBLICAL WORDS AND THEIR MEANING: An Introduction to Lexical Semantics.* Cambridge, OH: Christian Publishing House.

Andrews, E. D. (2025). *CAN WE TRUST THE BIBLE?* Cambridge, OH: Christian Publishing House.

Andrews, E. D. (2025). *DISCOVERING GENESIS ANSWERS: Exploring the Historical and Cultural Contexts of Genesis, One Insight at a Time (Answers from Genesis).* Cambridge, OH: Christian Publishing House.

Andrews, E. D. (2025). *DISCOVERING GENESIS ANSWERS: Tackling Tough Questions in Genesis: One Solution at a Time (Answers from Genesis).* Cambridge, OH: Christian Publishing House.

Andrews, E. D. (2025). *DISCOVERING GENESIS ANSWERS: Unveiling the Truths of Creation, One Answer at a Time (Answers from Genesis).* Cambridge, OH: Chritian Publishing House.

Andrews, E. D. (2025). *ISLAMIC IDEOLOGICAL JIHAD: Islamic-Funded, Islamic-Indoctrinated, Western Youth.* Cambridge, OH: Christian Publishing House.

Andrews, E. D. (2025). *LINGUISTICS AND THE BIBLICAL TEXT: Unlocking Scripture Through the Science of Language.* Cambridge, OH: Christian Publishing House.

Andrews, E. D. (2025). *OVERCOMING BIBLE DIFFICULTIES: Answers to the So-Called*

Errors and Contradictions [Second Edition]. Cambridge: Christian Publishing House.

Andrews, E. D. (2025). *PROVING GOD'S EXISTENCE.* Cambridge, OH: Christian Publishing House.

Andrews, E. D. (2025). *THE FACES OF ISLAM: Faith or Facade: Decoding Islam's Strategies.* Cambridge, OH: Christian Publishing House.

Andrews, E. D. (2025). *UNDERSTANDING BIBLICAL WORDS: A Guide to Sound Interpretation.* Cambridge, OH: Christian Publishing House.

Andrews, E. D. (2025). *WONDERFULLY MADE: Wonderful Are God's Works.* Cambridge, OH: Christian Publishing House.

www.ingramcontent.com/pod-product-compliance
Lightning Source LLC
LaVergne TN
LVHW020928090426
835512LV00020B/3255